DOUBLE

WEDDING RING

QUILTS

New Qui *DISCARD* *ld* *Favorite*

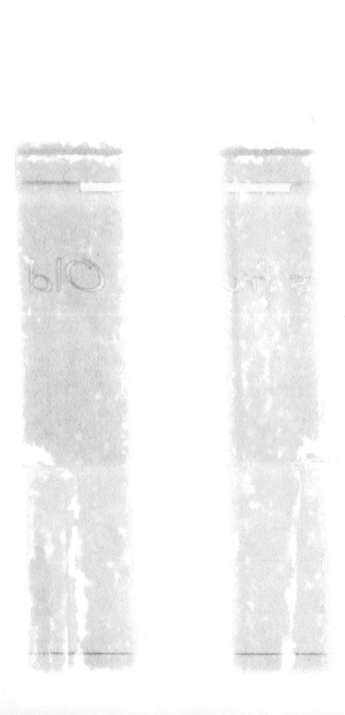

DOUBLE WEDDING RING QUILTS

New Quilts from an Old Favorite

Edited by Victoria Faoro

American Quilter's Society

P.O. Box 3290, Paducah, KY 42003-3290

Library of Congress Cataloging-in-Publication Data

Double wedding ring: new quilts from an old favorite.
p.   cm.
Includes index.
ISBN 0-89145-838-7: $14.95
1. Quilting – Patterns. 2. Appliqué – Patterns. 3. Double wedding ring quilts.
I. American Quilter's Society.
TT835.D69   1994   94-10943
746.9'7–dc20   CIP

Additional copies of this book may be ordered from:

American Quilter's Society
P.O. Box 3290
Paducah, KY 42002-3290

@$14.95. Add $1.00 for postage & handling.

Dedication

This book is dedicated to quiltmakers
of all times and all places, whose works
continue to inspire and delight.

Table of Contents

FOREWORD _____ 8

THE SPONSORS _____ 9

THE CONTEST _____ 10

THE WINNERS AND THEIR QUILTS _____ 12

    Log Cabin Double Wedding Ring – *Keiko Goke* _____ 14

    Wedding Ring Mosaics – *Nancy Lambert* _____ 16

    Hidden Passion – *Susan Stein* _____ 18

    An Ever-Fixed Mark – *Marilyn Henrion* _____ 20

    Leprechaun Wedding – *Deanna Deason Dison* _____ 22

    Agony and Ecstasy – *Shirley Robinson Davis* _____ 24

    He Was a Kansas Sunflower,
    She Was a Missouri Daisy – *Mildred Dort* _____ 26

    Tarantella – *Sylvia H. Einstein* _____ 28

    Indian Summer – *Sharon Gilmore-Thompson* _____ 30

    This Is NOT My Grandmother's Wedding Ring,
    It Is a NEW Generation of Quilts! – *Dianne S. Hire* _____ 32

    Rings of the 90's – *Sara Newberg King* _____ 34

    Citrus Circuit – *Jane Lloyd* _____ 36

    Japan in the Ancient Mirror – *Emiko Nagai* _____ 38

    Shotgun Wedding – *Marion Ongerth* _____ 40

    Royal Wedding – *Pieceful Scrappers* _____ 42

    It's Not All Hearts & Flowers – *Dorothy Stapleton* _____ 44

    Medley – *Elsie Vredenburg* _____ 46

    Attic Windows of My Mind – *Edith Zimmer* _____ 48

DOUBLE WEDDING RING TEMPLATES _____ 50

    8" Block _____ 51

    10" Block _____ 52

    12" Block _____ 53

14" Block _____ 54

16" Block _____ 56

18" Block _____ 58

WORKING WITH THE DESIGN – Tips & Tricks _____ 60

Curved Piecing *by Shirley Robinson Davis* _____ 60

Paper Piecing Rings *by Dianne S. Hire* _____ 61

An Old Pattern with a New Ring *by Susan Stein* _____ 62

In Search of a Design *by Keiko Goke* _____ 64

Shibori for Quilters *by Sara Newberg King* _____ 65

Planning Fabric Grain for Mosaics *by Nancy Lambert* _____ 68

PATTERNS FROM THE QUILTS _____ 70

Royal Wedding Block *by Pieceful Scrappers* _____ 70

Medley *by Elsie Vredenberg* _____ 72

Tarantella *by Sylvia H. Einstein* _____ 77

An Ever-Fixed Mark *by Marilyn Henrion* _____ 82

Leprechaun Wedding *by Deanna Deason Dison* _____ 85

Three-Dimensional Wedding Ring *by Edith Zimmer* _____ 90

Star Designs *by Mildred Dort* _____ 100

Kansas Sunflower _____ 100

Mariner's Compass _____ 101

Missouri Daisy _____ 102

Pinwheel _____ 103

Rolling Echoes; Carpenter's Puzzle _____ 104

Quilting Designs *by Emiko Nagai* _____ 105

INDEX OF QUILTMAKERS _____ 108

INDEX OF QUILTS _____ 109

THE MUSEUM _____ 110

Foreword

This book has been developed in conjunction with a Museum of the American Quilter's Society (MAQS) contest and exhibit entitled "New Quilts from Old Favorites." Dedicated to honoring today's quilter, MAQS has created this contest to recognize and share with others the fascinating array of interpretations that can grow out of a single traditional quilt pattern.

A brief introduction to the contest is followed by a presentation of the 18 finalists, including the five winners of awards. Full color photographs of the quilts are accompanied by their makers' comments, which provide fascinating insights. Full-size templates for the traditional pattern enable anyone to make a Double Wedding Ring quilt, minus the headache of drafting templates. The tips, techniques, and patterns contributed by the winning contestants make a wide range of quilts easier to execute in fabric.

It is our hope that this combination of outstanding quilts, full-size patterns, and instructional information will inspire as many outstanding quilts as the original contest did – adding new contributions to this pattern's continuing tradition.

The Sponsors

A special thanks goes to the corporations whose generous support has made this contest, exhibit, and book possible:

FABRIC TRADITIONS

NEW HOME®

The Contest

This publication grows out of an annual international contest sponsored by the Museum of the American Quilter's Society. Entitled "New Quilts from Old Favorites," this contest encourages quiltmakers to develop innovative quilts using a different traditional pattern each year. The theme for 1993 was the traditional Double Wedding Ring pattern, a long-time favorite for both individuals and the producers of commercial patterns.

The only design requirement for quilts entered in the contest was that the quilt be recognizable in some way as related to the Double Wedding Ring pattern. The quilt also had to be a minimum of 50" in each dimension and not exceed 100" in any one dimension, and it had to be quilted. A quilt could only be entered by the person who made it, and had to have been completed after December 31, 1988. Submitted from around the world were many exciting interpretations of this traditional pattern. From these entries were selected the 18 quilts featured in both this publication and the traveling exhibition.

The Double Wedding Ring pattern, with its curved interlocking circles, offers shapes and spaces different from those found in most pieced patterns. Some quilters find the prospect of piecing its many curves and angles intimidating and tell of avoiding use of the pattern. Others discover they find the very same components challenging.

In some cases the quilts entered in this contest were projects that had already been underway at the time the contest was announced; in other cases they had already been completed. The

Double Wedding Ring

Double Wedding Ring pattern is one quiltmakers often turn to when they are making a quilt to commemorate a special person or occasion.

A number of quilts entered in the competition were inspired by the contest theme. Many quilters commented that they had always intended to make a quilt based on the Double Wedding Ring pattern, but had never actually done it. This contest provided just the incentive they needed to make one. Still other quilts were the results of a combination of the desire to enter the contest and a desire to commemorate a special anniversary.

In at least one case the pattern is one that the quiltmaker has been exploring for a period of time, and several winners have remarked that they have found the Double Wedding Ring pattern so interesting that they are in the midst of a new series of quilts, all based on that pattern. In this book you will find comments from each of the winners, illustrating the variety of experiences and reactions these individuals had to working with this popular traditional pattern.

Some of the quilters have retained much from the traditional design, modifying only slightly the pieced structure and usual use of the design. Other quilters have boldly moved in new directions, re-interpreting the design quite dramatically. The quilts are a wonderful reminder of the latitude that traditional patterns offer quiltmakers. These patterns are there to be followed to whatever degree the maker wishes. And regardless of the degree of modification, the results can be very spectacular.

The Winners

KEIKO GOKE
Sendai, Miyagi, Japan
LOG CABIN DOUBLE WEDDING RING

NANCY LAMBERT
Mequon, Wisconsin
WEDDING RING MOSAIC

SUSAN STEIN
St. Paul, Minnesota
HIDDEN PASSION

MARILYN HENRION
New York, New York
AN EVER-FIXED MARK

DEANNA DEASON DISON
Spearsville, Louisiana
LEPRECHAUN WEDDING

And Their Quilts

SHIRLEY ROBINSON DAVIS

MILDRED DORT

SYLVIA H. EINSTEIN

SHARON GILMORE-THOMPSON

DIANNE S. HIRE

SARA NEWBERG KING

JANE LLOYD

EMIKO NAGAI

MARION ONGERTH

PIECEFUL SCRAPPERS

DOROTHY STAPLETON

ELSIE VREDENBURG

EDITH ZIMMER

FIRST
PLACE

LOG CABIN DOUBLE WEDDING RING

Cottons; 62" x 62"

Machine pieced, hand quilted & hand appliquéd

Keiko Goke

SENDAI, MIYAGI, JAPAN

MY QUILTMAKING

I began making quilts over 20 years ago, and I am very thankful that many American quilters share my interest in making them.

When I first began, I made quilts with traditional patterns, the way that many quilters do. I made quilts for beds, and was very happy to see members of my family using them.

As I continued to make quilts, I found the next thing I wanted to do was make a quilt that was a little different, a quilt that was something original. Little by little I experimented with my own designs.

I have always liked to draw. For me, making a quilt in fabric is like drawing or painting a picture. The fabrics are the paints and the needle is my brush. Now I find I just can't stop making quilts.

MY DOUBLE WEDDING RING QUILT

Recently I have enjoyed working with a template-free version of the Log Cabin pattern and have made many quilts using this traditional design. I love a number of other traditional patterns, including the Double Wedding Ring pattern, a design loved by many people.

I always thought that this traditional pattern was very lovely, but since it is a little difficult to make in the usual way, I had never used it in a quilt. I had only used the pattern in some smaller projects like bags and pouches.

I finally decided I would try to make a Double Wedding Ring quilt. However, I felt I didn't want to make mine in the traditional style. To design my quilt, I drew a Double Wedding Ring design freehand and used just a few of the lines.

People expect a Double Wedding Ring quilt to include many connected rings, but mine includes just one small part of the traditional design, greatly enlarged.

LOG CABIN DOUBLE WEDDING RING is an entirely original design. I think of it as a Double Wedding Ring done my own way.

People will probably be surprised to see my Double Wedding Ring Quilt, which includes just one section of the traditional design.

See page 64 for design ideas.

WEDDING RING MOSAICS

Cottons; 59" x 59"

Machine appliquéd & machine quilted

Nancy Lambert

MEQUON, WI

MY QUILTMAKING

While employed at my first job, I fell in love with an antique quilt but could not afford to buy it. I decided to make my own quilt, using skills I had developed sewing clothing.

A class later introduced me to appliqué, which I loved, and I began making traditional hand appliquéd quilts. When I bought a new sewing machine several years ago, I began working with machine appliqué and found I really liked the contemporary look it produces, especially when specialty threads are used.

Fortunately, in the quilting world machine work has become more acceptable. Recently I became a mother, which has been a great joy, but has meant that now there are definitely not enough hours in the day. Part of the challenge of entering the MAQS contest was finding the time to finish the quilt!

MY DOUBLE WEDDING RING QUILT

I thoroughly enjoyed working with the Double Wedding Ring design. I began by playing around with the pattern. When I'm designing, I make photocopy enlargements and reductions and experiment with them.

I designed this Double Wedding Ring quilt while I was pregnant. As I wanted to work on a design with smaller pieces, I especially investigated what I could do to make the pattern smaller.

I experimented with the pattern, modifying its size and looking at it from different angles. Out of these investigations came the idea of separate little pieces. I'm an engineer by training, which may explain the angles and small pieces.

This quilt is the first mosaic I have ever done. It's unusual for me to even work with a pieced design. If I had to count, I would probably be very surprised at the number of tiny squares. They took forever to cut and stitch.

This quilt was a lot of fun, and it also challenged me to grow as a quiltmaker.

> I really liked the circular nature of the Double Wedding Ring pattern and the way that a second pattern is formed by the rings.

See page 68-69 for tips on using fabric grain in mosaics.

THIRD PLACE

HIDDEN PASSION

Cottons; 51" x 62"

Machine pieced, machine appliquéd & machine quilted

Susan Stein

ST. PAUL, MN

MY QUILTMAKING

I actually make a quilt every week or two because I teach often and always update my samples. I started quilting in 1977, around the time of the bicentennial. I immediately became obsessed, and since then I have never been without a wide range of projects going, many classes to teach, and a variety of trips planned.

Recently I have specialized in making Double Wedding Ring quilts. This is probably my twentieth in a series that began when a shop owner I was working for asked me to try using Sharlene Jorgenson's Quick Strip template system.

Soon I was teaching classes and making a different quilt for each one. I made ones that included weaving through the background, appliquéd backgrounds, and all sorts of effects with hand-dyed fabrics. I always carry a design one step farther, so it remains traditional, but is a little different. Quilting always offers something new to try.

MY DOUBLE WEDDING RING QUILT

In HIDDEN PASSION I wanted to use gradations differently from the way they are normally used. In my grid, color changes from light to dark across the quilt, so some of the strips are pieced. Along with the Cherrywood® gradations I also used an over-dyed Hoffman® fabric, with the "hot" parts at the bottom so it looks as if there were flames at the bottom and cooler colors at the top.

This quilt also includes raw edged appliqué, which surprises some people. I invariably hear, "Oh, you can do that?" Appliqué suddenly appeals to more people. There is nothing wrong with turning edges under, but raw edges add texture and produce the bold contemporary look I aim for.

A little metallic thread contributes a fiery touch to the quilt, and as I was quilting I added orange squares to look like sparks. Creating a quilt is very exciting. You can't easily do a mockup, so the final quilt is always a surprise.

Though I've made hundreds of quilts, I still find it fascinating the way fabrics work when they're pieced together.

See page 62-63 for other design ideas.

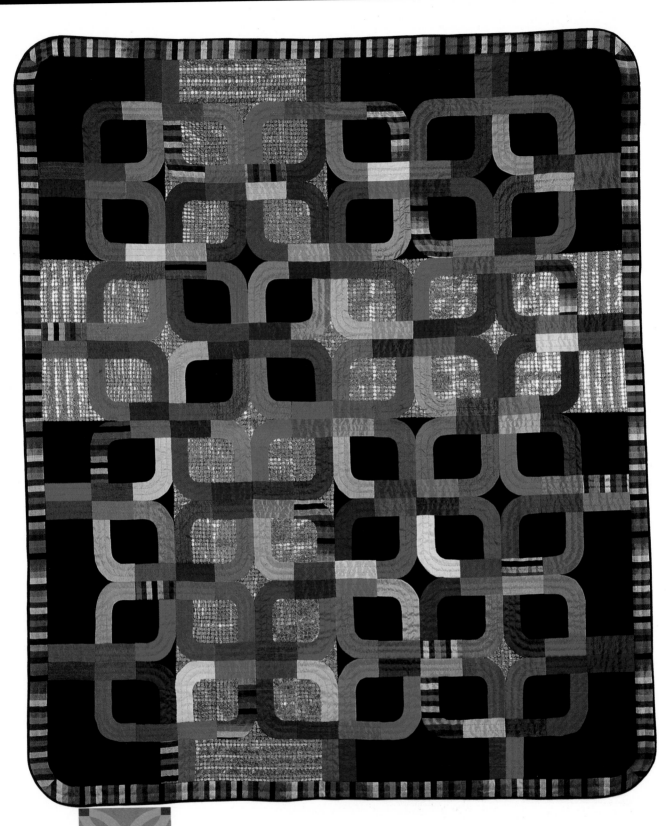

AN EVER-FIXED MARK

Silks, cottons, reflective synthetic; 51" x 60"

Machine pieced & hand quilted

Marilyn Henrion

NEW YORK, NY

MY QUILTMAKING

Quilting brings together everything I love: fabric, color, mathematics, design, poetry, music. I find there is no end to my satisfaction with making quilts.

I started making them as legacies for my four children, to leave something of me when I'm gone. Self-taught, I learned from magazines like *American Quilter*. My background was in graphic design, so the design training was there, but the techniques I learned from publications. I had been quilting for 12 years before I took a workshop.

MY DOUBLE WEDDING RING QUILT

When this MAQS competition was announced, I decided to develop an adaptation of the first original design quilt I had made. Working with this Double Wedding Ring style design also seemed a nice way to celebrate the fact that as of 1993 my husband and I had been married 41 years.

I liked working with the Double Wedding Ring design – it's complex enough to keep me interested. Machine piecing the curves takes a bit of practice, but once you've stitched a number of them you become quite adept.

One of the more difficult things about making this quilt was the fabric. The silk I used tended to fray easily, so when I was piecing the curves and flipping them, there was fraying. I had to be a little more careful than with cotton.

I was surprised to discover that the reflective synthetic fabric included in this quilt could be pieced. It's actually a knit fabric with circles glued on so strongly that they are an integral part of the fabric. Seeing the fabric on the bolt, I was so excited that I bought it not knowing whether or not it would work in a quilt. The fabric required a little extra care, but I was able to stitch right through the little circles, and could even hand quilt between them.

Working with that unusual fabric has made me want to experiment more with different types of fabric. At the moment I am quilting a piece made of linen, and I find myself wondering why this fabric hasn't been used more in quilts. It is exciting to consider all of the other fabrics that could be used.

Right now what is of great interest to me is experimenting with fabrics that would not normally be used in quilting.

See pages 82-84 for full-size patterns.

LEPRECHAUN WEDDING

Cottons; 72" x 84"

Machine pieced & hand quilted

Deanna Deason Dison

SPEARSVILLE, LA

MY QUILTMAKING

As a teenager I helped mother make quilts, and once married, I made them for use. But I'm actually very much an outdoors person. In college I studied landscape design, and later completed an M.A. in botany. I opened a flower shop and later a greenhouse, where I raised foliage plants until 1988.

I live in the country and spend much time working in the yard. People who know me are sometimes surprised to discover that I spend a lot of time sitting at a sewing machine inside. Presently, I help my auctioneer husband on Saturdays, and the rest of the time I am able to quilt.

I go to every class, lecture, and quilt show I can, and I also spend much time reading books to keep up with new developments in the field. There is always something to learn.

MY DOUBLE WEDDING RING QUILT

I made a traditional Double Wedding Ring scrap quilt for my daughter when she married in 1978, and in 1988, I made a Pickle Dish. With LEPRECHAUN WEDDING I wanted to work with the Double Wedding Ring pattern in a less traditional way.

I drew the quilt until it was just what I wanted. Then I had copies made and colored them in. While I was coloring, my very active four-year-old granddaughter talked on and on about a leprechaun. Another of my granddaughters had passed away in 1992, so my quilts made during that period had been sad. My four-year-old granddaughter's activity lifted my spirits, and this quilt became a happier project.

The quilt was a challenge to construct. I had the 4" and 8" blocks all laid out on the bed when my kittens got on the bed and scrambled everything. It took another three hours to lay it out again.

Looking at the quilt now, it's not a sad quilt, but it *was* made during the saddest part of my life.

I was afraid I wouldn't have time to make a Double Wedding Ring, but I decided to try. I finished it in six weeks!

See pages 85-89 for full-size patterns.

FINALIST

AGONY AND ECSTASY

Cottons; 53.25" x 53.25"

Machine pieced & machine quilted

Shirley Robinson Davis

PRESCOTT, AZ

MY QUILTMAKING

I was a professional rodeo photographer, but when we moved, I was suddenly too far away from my work to continue. My sister-in-law suggested I take a quilting class, and reluctantly I did. I immediately "got hooked" and have abandoned photography completely. Relocated in Arizona, I taught in a shop for a period. I like to design and make controlled but original art quilts.

I like machine quilting because it allows me to get quilts done – my machine is a best friend. I really enjoy looking at hand quilting, but my attention span just doesn't last long enough for me to hand quilt my work.

My husband is surprised I have stuck with quilting so long. I tend to jump around with many things, but, I have so many fabrics I will probably have to stick with this.

MY DOUBLE WEDDING RING QUILT

When I left Nevada, the quilt shop owners there gave me John Flynn's patterns. With our 40th anniversary coming up, I decided a Double Wedding Ring quilt would be a good present for my husband. In making that Southwestern theme Double Wedding Ring quilt, I found John Flynn's method so easy that I had no hesitation about making another quilt in this pattern.

When I began AGONY AND ECSTASY, I knew I didn't want an ordinary ring; I wanted it shaded. With no particular design in mind, I just started cutting fabric and putting it on my design wall. I cut pieces of hand-dyed sueded cottons from Cherrywood Quilts & Fabrics®, put them on the wall, stood back, and squinted. If the design didn't thrill me, I knew the piece wouldn't work.

The title came about because the quilt was such agony to make – I just kept cutting fabrics. I worked until the very last minute. My good friend Sharon, who is also in the exhibit, kept me working. If it hadn't been for her, I might never have finished.

I had always admired my grandmother's Double Wedding Ring quilt, but never felt I had the qualifications to make one myself.

See page 60 for construction tips.

25

HE WAS A KANSAS SUNFLOWER, SHE WAS A MISSOURI DAISY

Cottons; 70" x 80"

Hand appliquéd, hand pieced, & hand quilted

Mildred Dort

DUNEDIN, FL

MY QUILTMAKING

I had made a Sampler in the late 1970's, but I actively became involved with quiltmaking after retirement. When I retired in 1980, we move to Florida, where I joined a quilt club. I quickly became addicted, and now spend most of my time quilting.

I love fabric and just can't resist buying it every time I go into the store, and I find it very relaxing to sit and piece a quilt. I do most of my work by hand – everything is quilted by hand. Quilting allows me to use my artistic talents a bit; it provides a way to create things.

Usually I start with a traditional pattern and then modify the design to make something more contemporary. Lately my quilts have been combinations of piecing and appliqué, and often have been pictorial.

MY DOUBLE WEDDING RING QUILT

Prior to making this quilt I had completed one other Double Wedding Ring quilt, one with more traditional pieced rings. This quilt came about because September 1994 will mark our 50th wedding anniversary. I had already decided to make a quilt celebrating this occasion – the contest just helped the quilt come into being.

Another factor entered into its design as well. Our guild is having a show with the theme "A Parade of Stars," so I decided to use stars for the centers of my quilt's rings. Making the Double Wedding Ring pattern wasn't nearly as difficult as redrafting each star pattern to fit a 6¼" square.

This quilt was quite different from my other Double Wedding Ring quilt. Not only did I use solid fabric for the rings, but I also made a medallion-style quilt instead of using the pattern over all of the surface.

To finish off the quilt, I used trapunto to add the years – 1944 and 1994 – and the words "50th anniversary."

The Double Wedding Ring is a popular pattern, and was one of my early favorites. I put off making one because the pattern looked so difficult. It wasn't!

See pages 100-104 for full-size patterns for five of the stars.

TARANTELLA
Cottons; 53" x 53"

Machine pieced, machine quilted

Sylvia H. Einstein

BELMONT, MA

MY QUILTMAKING

I have been quilting ever since I made my first quilt in 1975 using a book by Jean Ray Laury. For that first project I chose an appliquéd design because I am not precise by nature, but I afterwards became so intrigued with the effect of pieced work that I have never made another appliquéd quilt.

There is much in quiltmaking that I like – the play of the colors, the way lines appear and reappear when you piece quilts with large patterned fabrics, the elements of chance. I enjoy both the limits pieced work gives me, and the way I can push and play with them in a quilt.

I am Swiss by birth and upbringing, but have lived in the United States since 1965. I have exhibited my quilts in the United States, twice in Quilt National, and in South America, Japan, and Europe. I teach and lecture here and in Europe. Quilting is for me a tribute to the beauty and resilience of the human spirit. It has become the focus of my life and the connection between my European and American selves.

MY DOUBLE WEDDING RING QUILT

This competition gave me an opportunity to work with a pattern I had never worked with before. I like traditional patterns very much and feel there is a great deal that can be done with them.

While working with the Double Wedding Ring pattern, I discovered that if I unbalanced the rings I could do interesting things. When the rings are the same width, nothing happens when the block is rotated, but if a fat ring and a thin ring are used, movement can be achieved. I drafted the "unbalanced" pattern on my computer, copied it, and cut it apart.

A friend gave me 10 yards of a 1960's Marimekko® fabric she had found at a garage sale. I cut the rings from that fabric, pinned them to the wall, and then added other fabrics that looked good with the wild 1960's fabric.

The grays drained a little of the energy of the wild print, which was good. It was too overwhelming on its own. It always takes a while to find the right combinations.

Using uneven rings opens the block up to experimentation. I'm now on my third quilt inspired by this traditional block. It's the first time I have ever made quilts in a series.

See pages 77-81 for full-size patterns.

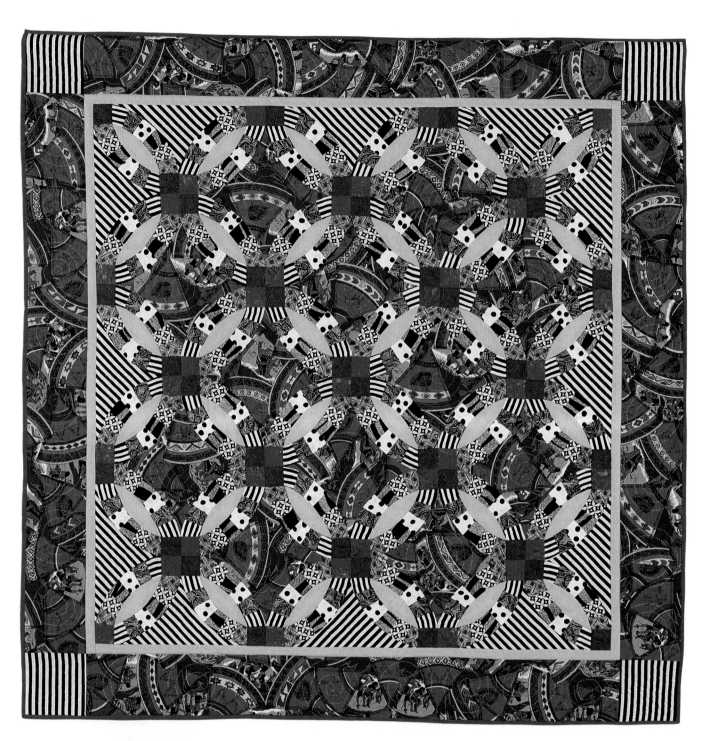

INDIAN SUMMER

Cottons; 65" x 65"

Machine pieced, hand & machine quilted

Sharon Gilmore-Thompson

LAMOILLE, NV

MY QUILTMAKING

When we relocated to northern Nevada about ten years ago, I wasn't working and took a quilt class at the local community college. I became fascinated by quilting and couldn't get enough. I had always loved fabric and had sewn for family and friends. Today, I concentrate exclusively on quilting. I have been quilting full-time for nearly a year, hoping to make it a successful business.

I'm the "bizarre" quiltmaker here in northern Nevada. I like the contemporary effect of mixing non-traditional prints with traditional patterns, which allows for creative interpretations of different themes. It amazes me that you can look at hundreds of quilts and no two will be the same. Being able to put so much of yourself into the work fascinates me.

MY DOUBLE WEDDING RING QUILT

I started INDIAN SUMMER knowing I was going to enter the MAQS contest. I began the quilt with black and white on the arc, later adding yellow. Then I started to experiment with different fabrics. I cut several before a teepee fabric I had bought on a sale table caught my eye. Once on my design wall, the fabric clearly was the zinger the quilt needed. The addition of the black and white striped fabric pulled the quilt together.

I hadn't worked with the Double Wedding Ring pattern before and was extremely intimidated by its insetting. But I found constructing the quilt was very challenging; I really loved making the pattern. I used John Flynn's template method and continue using it.

I enjoyed making this quilt so much that I couldn't leave it alone; I worked non-stop. I liked the pattern so much that I made a second and am now planning a group of twelve.

Without the contest I would probably never have worked with the Double Wedding Ring pattern – now I'm engrossed in it.

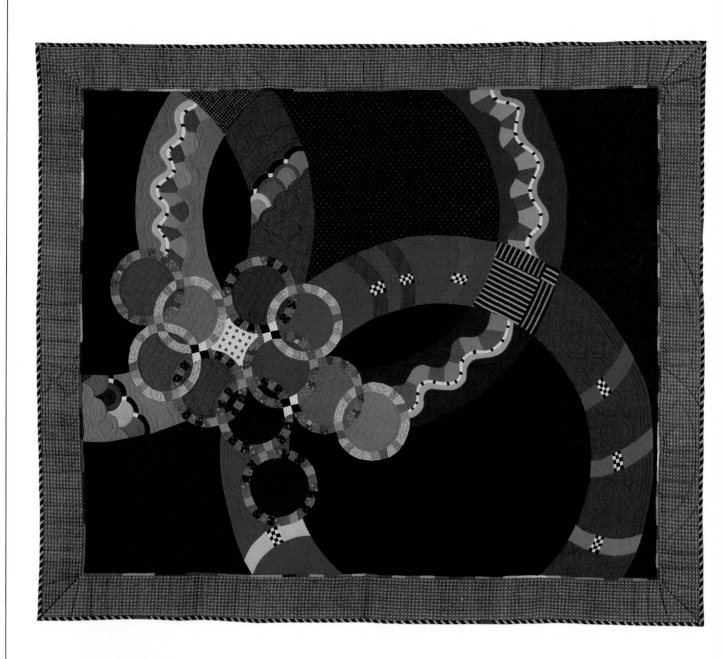

FINALIST

THIS IS NOT MY GRANDMOTHER'S WEDDING RING, IT IS A NEW GENERATION OF QUILTS!

Cottons, some hand-dyed; 70" x 58"

Hand & machine pieced, hand quilted

Dianne S. Hire

BELFAST, ME

MY QUILTMAKING

My husband says love of quilting must be genetic. Working with fiber gives me much satisfaction; I enjoy the tactile qualities, the color, the design. Before moving to Maine I spent 17 years in retailing as a buyer for clothing, so the sense of good design was there.

I moved from New Orleans to Maine, where I found what I most enjoy doing. Quilting "took" in a way that nothing else has. It surprises me how much I enjoy it.

My learning to quilt has much to do with my grandmother. When she was very ill, I traveled south to spend three weeks with her. She soon regained some of her strength, and before long began to ask for her box of "quilting." She would finger the tiny pieces, and then fall asleep, holding the box.

Having made clothing but never quilts, I asked "Mammy" to teach me to quilt. She suddenly lit up. I made four 10" blocks with her supervision and returned to Maine hooked on quilting.

MY DOUBLE WEDDING RING QUILT

My grandmother pieced quilts in the Double Wedding Ring design for each of her children and grandchildren. After she died, I wanted to do something in her honor.

I began making this, my first Double Wedding Ring quilt, by constructing 8" blocks in shades of "country" blue and yellow. The fabrics were beautiful together, but as the quilt progressed I became bored with it.

Finally I ripped out the yellow centers, splashed vibrant colors everywhere, and incorporated the 8" rings in 4' rings. Mammy's comment would surely have been, "It's certainly bright!" Her traditional freedom of expression launched me into a new abstraction of that freedom.

This quilt jars people, and makes them realize that there is much that can be done with the traditional pattern. I had great fun making this quilt to honor Pearl Whitaker, who loved to piece, but "didn't care much for quilting!"

My grandmother's favorite quilt pattern was the Double Wedding Ring. It was only natural to want to honor her with a quilt in this traditional pattern.

See page 61 for a piecing tip.

the destruction of a nation

stress can lead to growth or destruction

begins in its families

FINALIST

RINGS OF THE 90's

Cottons; 55" x 55"

Shibori, stenciling, machine pieced & quilted

Sara Newberg King

PINE ISLAND, MN

MY QUILTMAKING

As an occupational therapist, I have done many different crafts. After our 2½ year old daughter died in 1978, I walked up and down the aisles of a local craft store, wanting to make something in our daughter's memory. I decided that the time I would have given Erica I would give to making a quilt. The result was a cross stitch quilt, and Erica continues to lead me to quilting.

I no longer work as an occupational therapist. Instead, I teach quilting. When I had three teenagers at home, I found quilting was good therapy for me, and my students tell me it is for them. I think that is one reason many women have found it so appealing. We all need a creative outlet.

MY DOUBLE WEDDING RING QUILT

The inspiration for this quilt was the saying on its borders – I wanted to put it into a quilt. I mulled the possibilities over on trips last summer and then, when I read about the MAQS competition,

I realized it would be perfect to use that saying with the Double Wedding Ring design.

I also wanted to use the shibori technique, so I combined it with stenciling. I purposely created some squares with beautiful lines, and some with ugly lines.

I put the blocks together so that the design started in the top left corner with beautiful marriages, machine quilted with positive words about marriage. Towards the center, some of the bleach splotched around and the rings began to need attention. I purposely didn't stencil some of the rings here, so they would be broken. Children fall through broken rings on one block. At the bottom, where the shibori makes the fabric look ugly and without a pattern, I wrote the words that break up a marriage.

A saying at the bottom center of the quilt says, "Stress can lead to growth or destruction." A friend of mine who is divorced remarked on my having grown tremendously without having to divorce to do it. I thought that was a wonderful compliment to my husband. We have both grown. You don't have to break up your marriage to grow.

I think quilting is preventive therapy. We all need a creative outlet.

See pages 65-67 for shibori instructions.

CITRUS CIRCUIT

Cottons; 56" x 58"

Machine pieced, hand & machine quilted

Jane Lloyd

BALLYMENA, CO. ANTRIM, NORTHERN IRELAND

MY QUILTMAKING

I became involved in quilt making 17 years ago, wanting to express myself in a medium that was easy and did not need a lot of expensive equipment. In art college I had done everything from metal work to painting. I was very keen on geometric shapes and color, and all that seemed to really work well in fabric.

I joined the Northern Ireland Patchwork Guild and never looked back. It was good to find a group with the same interests.

I love the color and the feel of fabric. I usually start off with an idea, not thinking it all the way through, and work to see what will happen. The work just grows. I pin it on the wall and keep looking at it, to see if it could become more interesting.

It would be difficult for me to design a whole quilt and then make it; there would be no excitement along the way – the adrenaline would not be flowing. I don't even decide where I am going to place colors until I start. I just pick a selection with which I want to work, like a painter who mixes colors along the way.

MY DOUBLE WEDDING RING QUILT

The technique used in this quilt was string piecing by machine over paper. An *American Quilter* magazine article by Caryl Bryer Fallert on this technique (Vol. VI, No. 3) changed the way I construct quilts. I used to do everything by hand because I found it more accurate. Now I use this method and can make quilts much more quickly.

I had completed my first Double Wedding Ring quilt and wanted to do another. Then I saw the MAQS competition and decided to explore the design – I like a challenge.

I wanted to get away from the traditional design, so I played around with breaking it up. When I finally decided on my design, I photocopied it and pinned it to the wall. The next day I realized it was not a Double Wedding Ring but rather single rings, so I added the thin curved lines!

I am planning another Double Wedding Ring quilt with different thicknesses of strips. This design has great possibilities.

My husband just came in to make a sandwich and discovered there was no bread – this is what happens when one gets involved in patchwork!

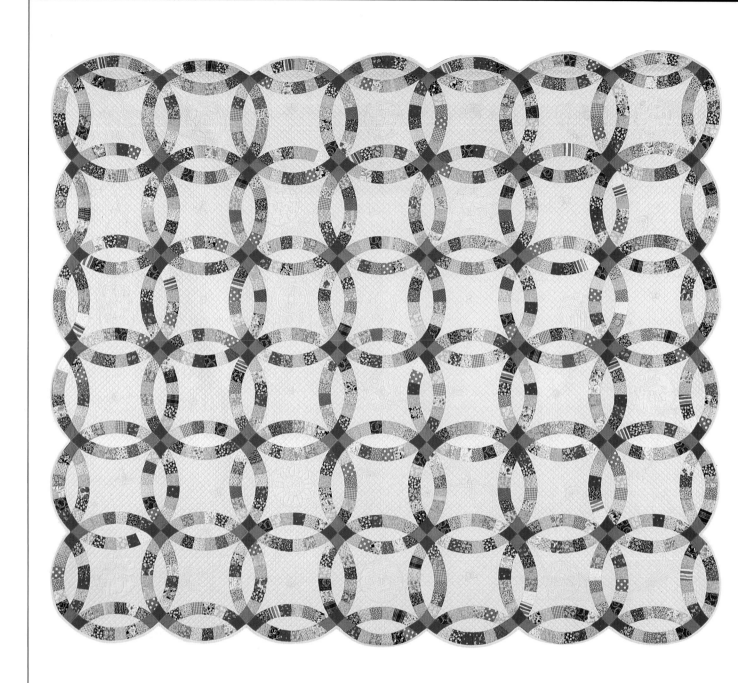

JAPAN IN THE ANCIENT MIRROR

Cottons; 80" x 94"

Hand pieced & quilted

Emiko Nagai

KASHIBA-SHI, NARA-KEN, JAPAN

MY QUILTMAKING

Quiltmaking is very popular in Japan. Exhibitions are often held in department stores and showrooms, and there are many workshops all over the country. Fifteen years ago I studied quiltmaking in a two-year workshop.

I am very interested in collecting textiles and handcrafting myself. When I read *Anne of Green Gables* by L.M. Montgomery and several stories written by Laura Ingalls Wilder, I wanted to know about the patchwork described in those stories. I studied and discovered the quilt. It is said that women in the United Stated began quiltmaking not just to save valuable cloth, but also to express affection and consideration for their families. Knowing that, I became involved with quiltmaking as a way to express myself.

I love Japanese tradition, and it has been a great influence on my quiltmaking. Japan has four seasons and life there is full of colors. My quiltmaking is influenced by those colors. Quiltmaking is like painting pictures, and each pattern has its own story. I make stories when I make quilts, and the strength of the stories makes me enjoy sewing.

MY DOUBLE WEDDING RING QUILT

In my quilt JAPAN IN THE ANCIENT MIRROR, I combined images of marriage and mirrors. I had heard that in the United States brides prepare something worked with the Double Wedding Ring pattern for their marriages. The mirror has been considered a precious art in Japan and was often used as a talisman to protect people from evil in ancient and medieval times. Japanese women have thought of mirrors as treasures in which their lives are reflected. Brides carry dresser mirrors into their new houses prior to any other furniture.

Because of the mystery and magic of mirrors, most are decorated with elaborate designs. I designed my quilt using patterns from the mirrors of Shosoin, a mid-eighth century treasure house, and those of medieval Dokyo. The braided cord called "kumihimo" is a symbol of good luck. I used fine-stitched Japanese embroidery to make the mirror designs and the braided cords stand out from the other quilting.

Next, I will work with the Double Wedding Ring pattern for my young niece when she gets married.

The Double Wedding Ring pattern reminds me of links in a chain and infinity. The links symbolize lasting relationships and the rings, perfection, harmony, and peace. In other words, the pattern is a symbol of never-ending happiness.

See pages 105-107 for full-size quilting patterns.

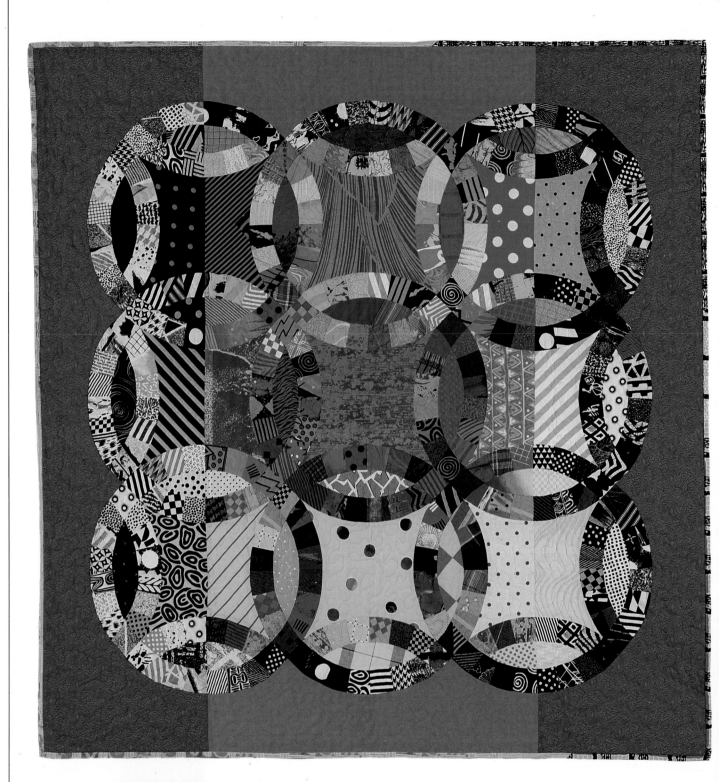

SHOTGUN WEDDING
Cottons, cotton blends, crossing guard fabric; 52" x 53"
Machine pieced & machine quilted

Marion Ongerth

BERKELEY, CA

MY QUILTMAKING

In 1981 I saw examples of student work from Roberta Horton's Amish class on the walls of a fabric store. I was immediately attracted to the bright colors and geometric shapes. It was my first exposure to the quilt as an art medium. Not being from a quilting background, I had a lot of skills to learn and took many classes before I began to work on original designs.

I studied graphic design in college and my primary interest is in manipulating color to heighten its tension and emotional impact. My inspiration comes from many sources including the works of the French impressionist painters and American blues and jazz improvisation. I design my quilts to be viewed vertically on the wall rather than horizontally on a bed.

Working with fabric is essential to me. We are wrapped in cloth at birth, live our lives surrounded by cloth, and are finally wrapped in cloth at death. By making my art in this medium I feel connected to something timeless and enduring.

MY DOUBLE WEDDING RING QUILT

When I think of the Double Wedding Ring pattern, I think of a white background with rings of 1930's housedress fabrics. I wanted my quilt to reflect the variety of fabrics available in the 1990's. I wanted it to be a record of my fabric collection.

For many years I have been working with the circle motif, the symbol of wholeness and the self. I wanted to honor the quilting tradition that inspired my art by designing a piece that married the traditional Double Wedding Ring pattern with the strong colors I love.

I challenge myself by posing color problems and finding solutions for them. I'm fascinated by the interplay of richly mixed colors that produce both emotional reaction and a rhythmic riot of colorful movement.

I designed my piece without much thought to background fabric and the challenge for me was to find one that was assertive enough to stand up to the strong colors in the rings. I solved my problem by using an orange polyester crossing guard fabric, the only orange I could find strong enough to balance the turquoise.

The title "Shotgun Wedding" came from nowhere – the outrageous orange just looked as if it had needed to be forced into the quilt.

41

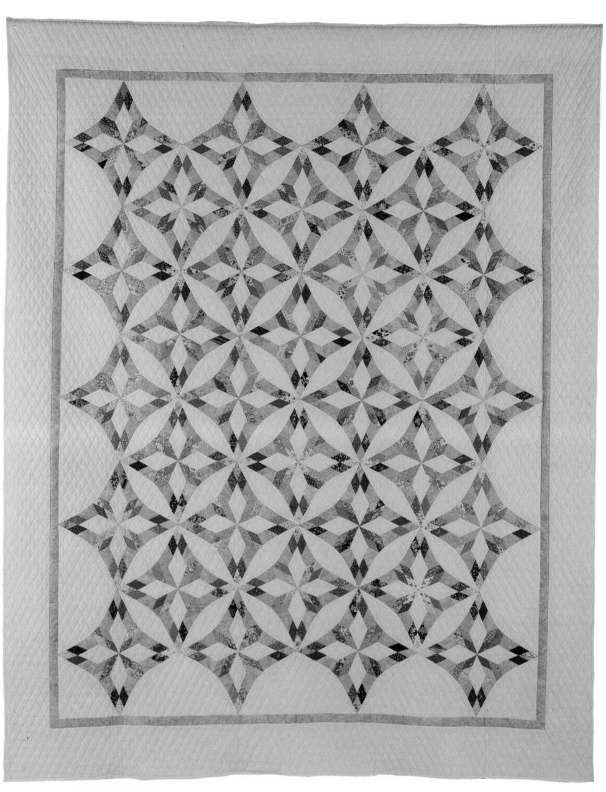

ROYAL WEDDING

Cottons; 84" x 100"

Hand & machine pieced, hand quilted

Pieceful Scrappers

Commentary by Lois Léger
WILLOWDALE, ONTARIO, CANADA

OUR QUILTMAKING

We began quilting together in 1986. There are now seven of us, and we all belong to York Heritage Guild, a large quilt guild in Toronto with over 400 members. Two of our members were charter members of that guild.

Drawn together by our mutual love of scrap quilts and the pleasure of working together on a large quilt frame, we meet every Wednesday to hand piece and hand quilt scrap quilts. I joined the group last, and have been quilting since 1985; most members have been quilting for 10 to 12 years.

We select a pattern, determine the number of blocks each member must do, and then all make our own blocks using our own fabrics. Usually there is one coordinating fabric we all use. Sometimes our quilts include bright colors or a dark background, but generally we tend to be pretty traditional.

OUR DOUBLE WEDDING RING QUILT

Competition wasn't really our goal when we started this quilt, but we have had much local success so we have tried to make each quilt a little more interesting, a little better than the last. This quilt is made in a pattern we call Royal Wedding.

This design was based on a traditional block for which a pattern was given in *Scraps Can Be Beautiful* by Jan Halgrimson (©1979, Weaver-Finch Publications, Edmonds, WA). We modified the pattern given for the traditional block which was called Chimney Swallows in that book and Coronation in Jinny Beyer's. Names with royal suggestions prompted our title for the modified block drafted by member Mary Lou Watson.

We had reservations about using this pattern, it was quite a challenge to piece. Some of us liked the challenge; others weren't too crazy about it. We were rewarded when we saw the quilt put together.

We had already started this quilt when we heard of the competition, and we felt this design would be perfect.

What probably surprises people most about this quilt is the fact that seven different people made it. The green was the only common fabric among the many blocks.

BACK: Barbara Pollock, Rhonda Penney, Marion Pilkington. FRONT: Mary Lou Watson, Lois Léger. ABSENT: Margaret Sneyd, Edyth Yeomans.

See pages 70-71 for full-size pattern.

IT'S NOT ALL HEARTS & FLOWERS

Miscellaneous household fabrics; 50" x 50"

Crazy patchwork with buttons & embroidery, hand quilted

Dorothy Stapleton

LEATHERHEAD, SURREY, ENGLAND

MY QUILTMAKING

I became involved in quiltmaking in 1980, after taking a class from an English woman who had just returned from the USA. She taught us American Patchwork – we thought it was always done over papers!

Incredibly thrifty, I cannot bear waste – the thought of creating works of art from nothing really appeals to me. I also love the idea of making useful works of art which will keep you warm.

I was previously a potter and a crafts teacher. I like quiltmaking above other crafts as it's portable and can be done while traveling or in odd moments without much mess. It keeps me sane as I mind my husband's office all week.

I have won ribbons for my quilts at The National Patchwork Championships, and Quilts U.K. Last year I won their cup for humor with my "I Hate Housework" quilt, a similar style quilt made from household dusters, dishcloths, and a napkin from the Ritz Hotel!

There should be more fun and laughs in quilting. I enjoy it when my quilts raise a smile.

MY DOUBLE WEDDING RING QUILT

I once made a Double Wedding Ring quilt with a friend and vowed never to do one again! When I think of the Double Wedding Ring pattern, I think of the fuss of the curves and decisions about what to do with the edges.

This design developed from a current interest in crazy quilts with embroidered writing. As it was my 30th wedding anniversary, I wanted to make a quilt about marriage for my husband. This design seemed an obvious choice.

The crazy patchwork was stitched by machine on pre-cut shapes of flannel sheeting. The plain centers were hand quilted, and embroidery was added to cover the raw edges. Sayings were marked with dried slivers of hardened soap and embroidered.

I didn't make this quilt for the competition but read about it after and thought I might enter. About to send the quilt, I discovered it was two inches too small. In a panic I added the stuffed hearts and embroidered flowers to bring it to size. They actually made it look better and tied in with the name and theme.

The title for my quilt came from an old aunt who on her husband's death wrote to say, "We were very happy, but it wasn't all hearts and flowers."

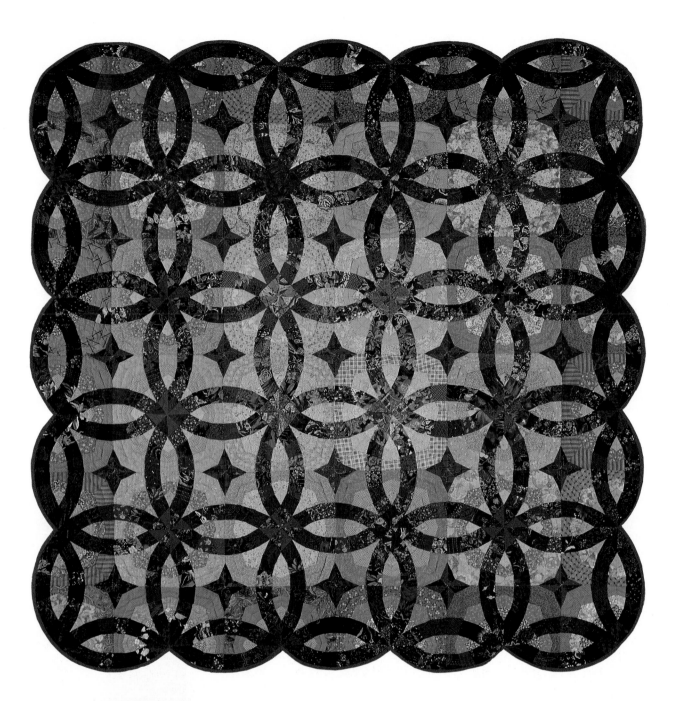

MEDLEY

Cottons; 63" x 63"

Machine pieced & machine quilted

Elsie Vredenburg

TUSTIN, MI

MY QUILTMAKING

My grandmother lived with us when I was in high school. She had pieced quilts all of her life, and one day announced that she and I were going to make a quilt. I had taken sewing in home economics, but wasn't overly enthusiastic about learning to quilt. My mother encouraged me to do it because Grandma needed to be needed; she was used to being busy. I filled the gap and got hooked on quilting. I didn't do much while my children were small, but the bicentennial brought me back to quilting. I made a small wallhanging to commemorate the event.

There is something in me that needs to create. I don't have an art background and hate to use the word artist, but there is an artist hidden in me that is trying to get out. It is the visual element of quilting that interests me most. I am visually attracted to quilts.

MY DOUBLE WEDDING RING QUILT

I've made lots of Double Wedding Ring quilts. In fact, the third quilt I ever made was a Double Wedding Ring, probably because my grandma had the pattern and it intrigued me. It's also a good quilt for using up little scraps. Almost every time I make one I say I will never make another. The pattern doesn't have the nice straight seams I like to work with. It's more challenging to get the quilt to lie flat.

Just before beginning this quilt I was working on another quilt in which I wanted to include some of my grandmother's patterns. One of these patterns was the Double Wedding Ring, but I didn't want to include any curves. As I tried to develop that pattern using angles rather than curves, I suddenly realized I could make a quilt for the MAQS contest.

I designed this block with no curved seams using the Electric Quilt® program, a computer program I've been working with for a year. The quilt is made of blocks that are square, and the background makes a second circle. Study is needed to understand how it went together.

I have sold quilts for years and am often asked how I can bear to part with a quilt after putting in so much time. That's never been a problem for me. I find more satisfaction in making them than I do in owning them.

See pages 72-76 for full-size patterns.

ATTIC WINDOWS OF MY MIND

Cottons; 77" x 93"

Machine pieced & hand quilted

Edith Zimmer

SAN DIEGO, CA

MY QUILTMAKING

My first quilt was a Lone Star made for my daughter's wedding. It was fashioned after a picture in a magazine. Having done dressmaking for years, I had the sewing skills but knew nothing about sandwiching quilts. I remember lying on the floor to pin the layers together and quilting it with buttonhole twist.

One of my first classes was based on the design element of quilting, and it inspired me to experiment with my own ideas. This put to good use my knowledge of geometry and a college drafting class I had taken earlier.

Growing up in Minnesota I had watched my mother make quilts. She made the Log Cabin, Grandmother's Flower Garden, and the Double Wedding Ring patterns. I was sure that someday I, too, would make quilts. I never dreamed that they would number in the hundreds.

MY DOUBLE WEDDING RING QUILT

For sentimental reasons I chose to duplicate my mother's quilts. I had postponed working with the Double Wedding Ring design, waiting for just the right idea which would make it uniquely mine.

When the AQS Quilt Show had the Attic Windows pattern as their special theme, I decided that I would try to combine the two patterns.

I have always enjoyed working with the three dimensional designs and was pleased with the results of this one.

The name of the quilt reflects a moment of insecurity in which I wondered whether the quilt would appear the same to others as it did to me.

When I began going to quilt shows, I realized that I had to become involved – I could express my ideas in quilts.

See pages 90-99 for full-size patterns for a similar quilt.

Double Wedding Ring Templates

Included in this section are full templates for the traditional Double Wedding Ring pattern in five different sizes. Select the size most appropriate for your fabrics and project plans and try your own hand at this popular pattern.

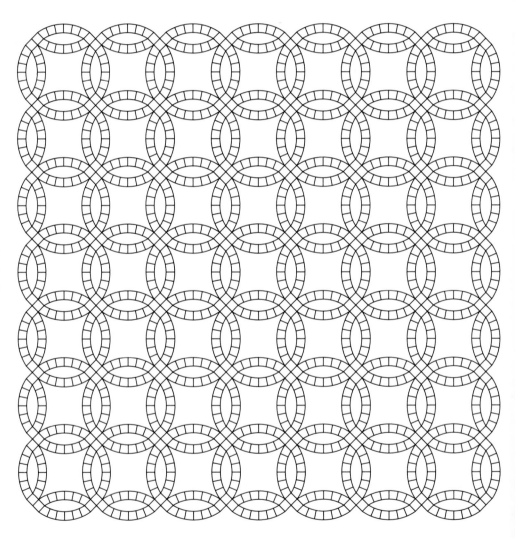

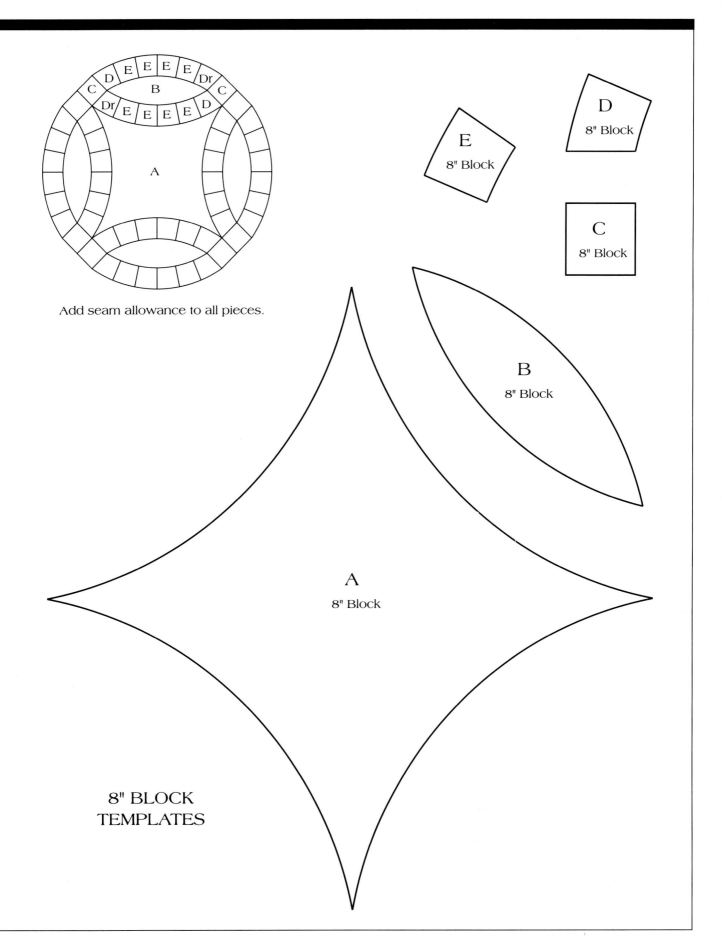

Add seam allowance to all pieces.

E
8" Block

D
8" Block

C
8" Block

B
8" Block

A
8" Block

8" BLOCK
TEMPLATES

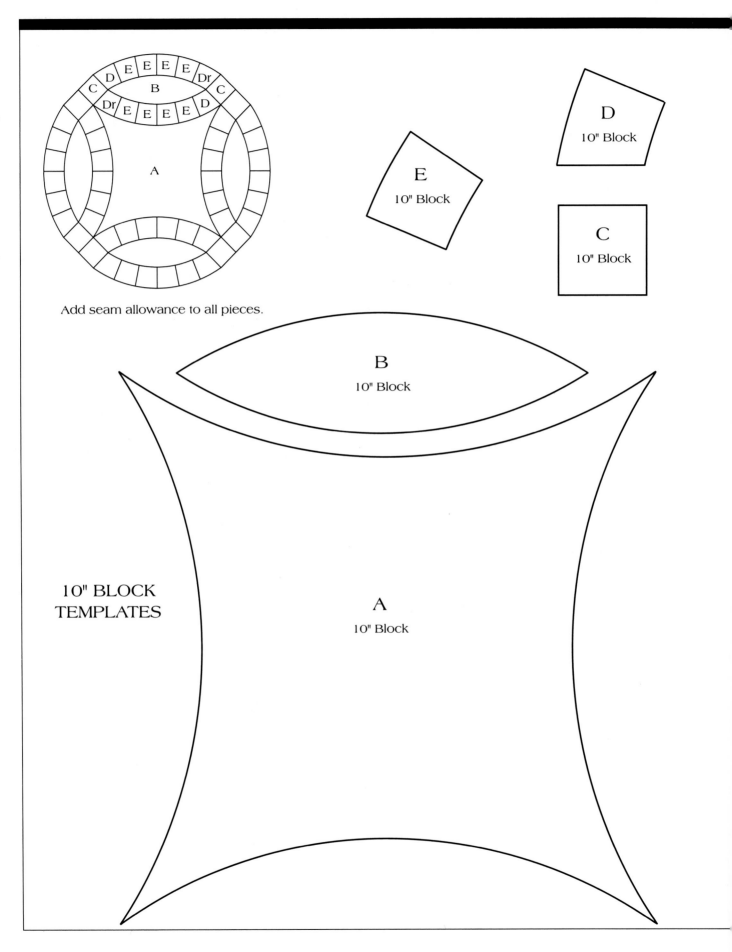

Add seam allowance to all pieces.

D
10" Block

E
10" Block

C
10" Block

B
10" Block

10" BLOCK
TEMPLATES

A
10" Block

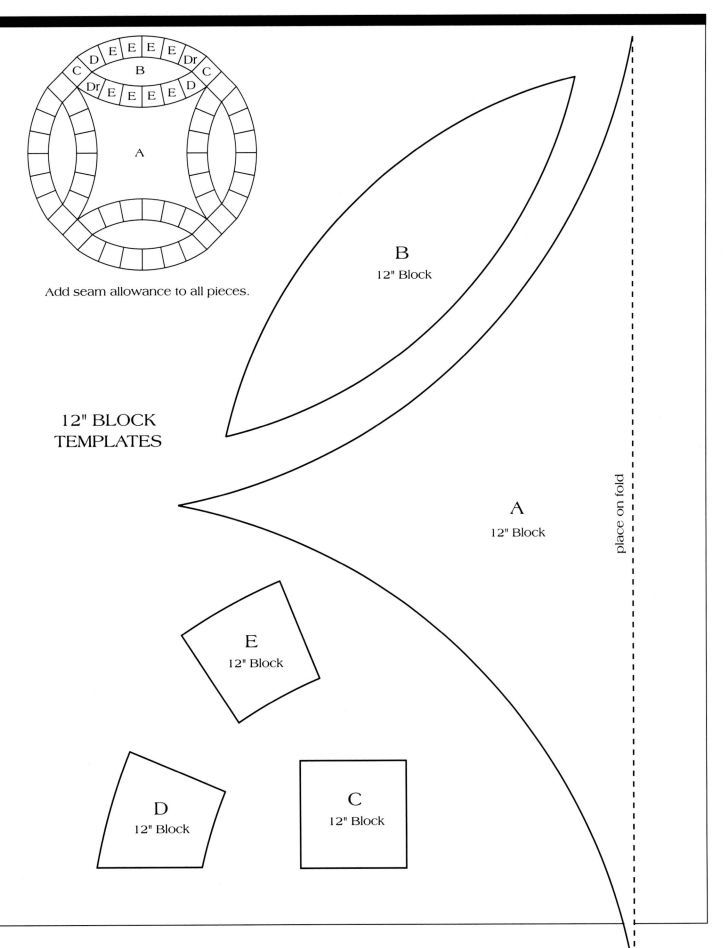

Add seam allowance to all pieces.

12" BLOCK
TEMPLATES

B
12" Block

A
12" Block

place on fold

E
12" Block

D
12" Block

C
12" Block

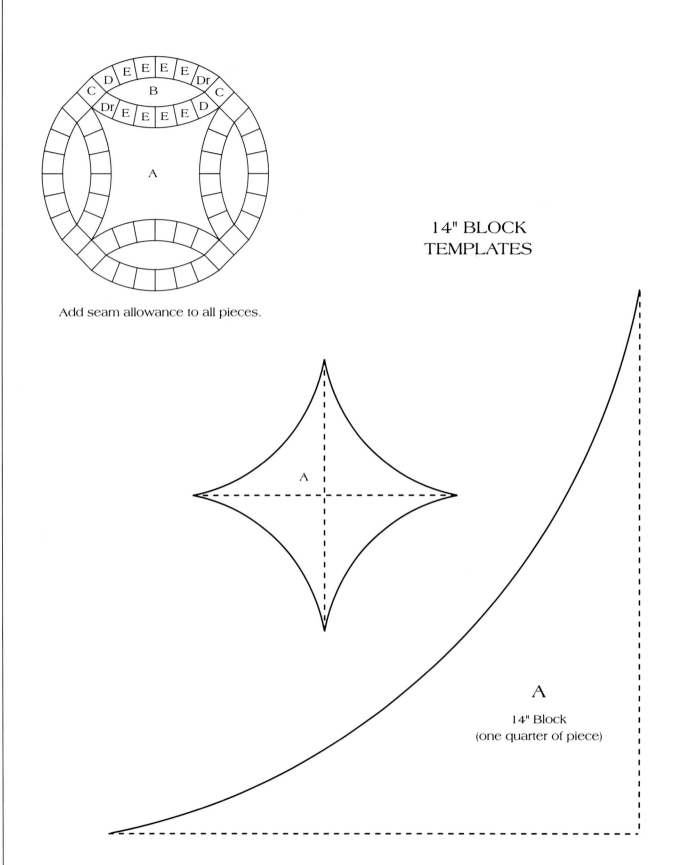

Add seam allowance to all pieces.

14" BLOCK
TEMPLATES

A

A
14" Block
(one quarter of piece)

Add seam allowance to all pieces.

14" BLOCK
TEMPLATES

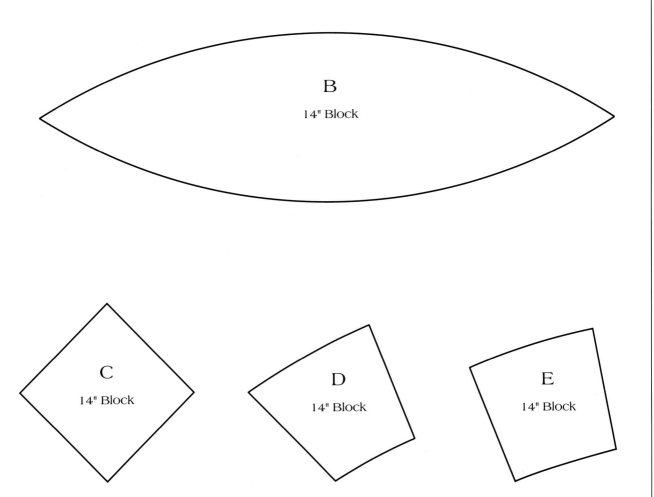

B

14" Block

C

14" Block

D

14" Block

E

14" Block

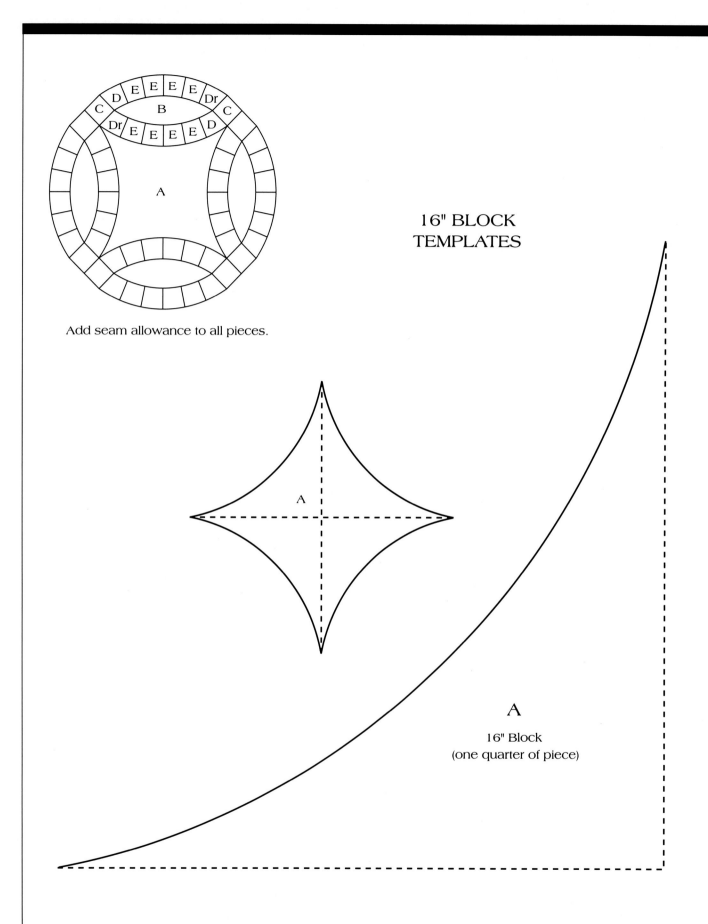

Add seam allowance to all pieces.

16" BLOCK
TEMPLATES

A

A
16" Block
(one quarter of piece)

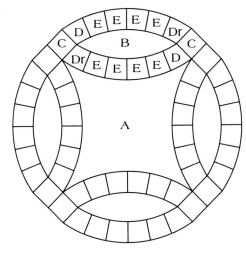

Add seam allowance to all pieces.

16" BLOCK
TEMPLATES

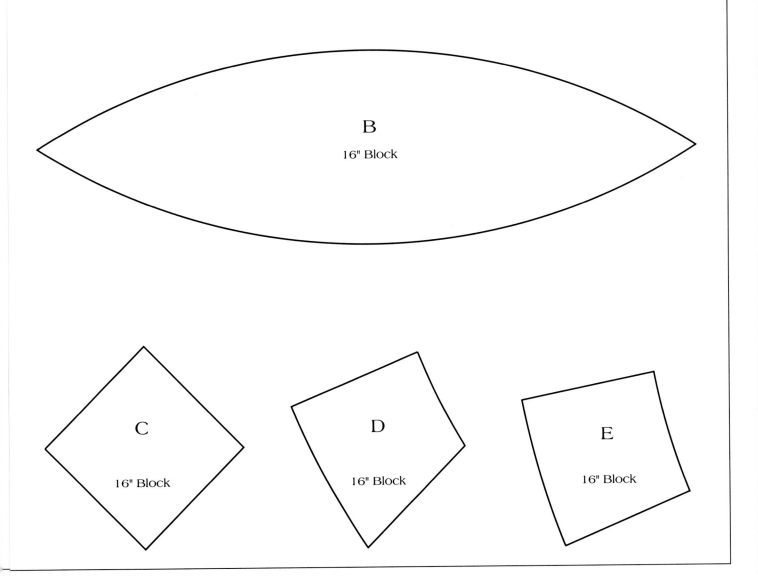

B
16" Block

C
16" Block

D
16" Block

E
16" Block

Working with the Design

TIPS & TRICKS

CURVED PIECING
BY SHIRLEY ROBINSON DAVIS

To get a perfect fit on curved pieces:

■ Fold the pieces in half and finger press at the center of the seam line. If desired also clip ⅛" into seam allowance or dot with a pencil mark at that point.

■ Clip ⅛" into the seam allowance of the *concave piece only*, along the entire curve. Fig. 1.

■ Place the concave (inside clipped piece) on top of the convex (outward curve) piece, matching center marks. Pin, starting in the center, matching ends, and then pinning in between. Fig. 2.

■ Sew with the concave piece on top, removing pins as you come to them. If you spread your hand on the piece and rotate the fabric as you sew, in one continuous motion, it will be easy to get a smooth seam. Fig. 3.

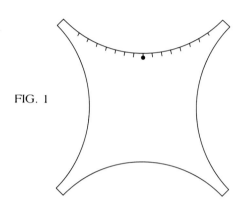

FIG. 1

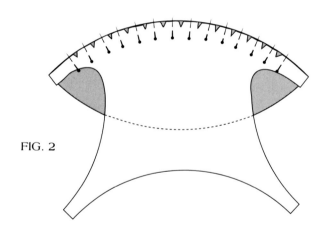

FIG. 2

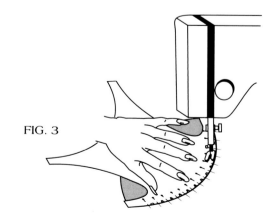

FIG. 3

PAPER PIECING RINGS
BY DIANNE S. HIRE

The 8" rings began as piecework for car trips. But, as the work progressed, I used Caryl Bryer Fallert's paper piecing method, as described in *American Quilter* (Fall 1990), for creating the rings in my quilt. I cut my drawing apart, stitched one fabric to a paper ring, flipped the fabric, added another, and so on.

Eventually I decided to incorporate several size rings, including larger four-foot rings. To create larger rings, I drew circles on paper, using a pencil attached to a string stabilized at the circle's center, a method learned in Girl Scouts.

I also paper-pieced a number of smaller 4" rings, thinking I would create a border with them. I actually made a much easier border, but I used a few of these rings to create backart. Paper piecing really works well with this design.

ABOVE: Front side of a section of paper-pieced 4" rings.

LEFT: Back side of the paper-pieced rings, with the paper still attached.

BUNNY TRAILS

PLAIDS AND STRIPES

SOUTHWESTERN

PHOTOS: MICHAEL KEEFE

ROSE RINGS

AN OLD PATTERN WITH A NEW RING
BY SUSAN STEIN

The Double Wedding Ring pattern is a favorite with quilters and non-quilters alike. Done in traditional fabrics it is warm and attractive; done in contemporary fabrics it can be very exciting and powerful. Susan Stein of St. Paul, MN, offers design tips and a few examples – other quilts of her own making.

■ Dyed gradations work well with the dark values either at the center or ends of the arcs, or going from light to dark across the arc.

■ The use of print fabrics in the rings can soften their effect.

■ The use of a large print in the background areas gives a different emphasis to the design. Use of solid arcs in different colors can complement a very bold print that needs no competition.

■ Contrasting colors, values, or prints work well for the wedges – too much blending will make the arcs look like one piece of fabric. Corner "squares" done in high contrast to the arcs can create an interesting secondary design.

BUNNY TRAILS, 38" x 48", 1990. A juvenile print was used for the background with colors for the arc and corner squares matched to the print. The layers were secured with colored buttons and quilted in the seam lines of the rings.

■ Plaids, cut with a template system, will look interesting because grain line will be random.

PLAIDS AND STRIPES, 42" x 52", 1990. For this quilt plaids and stripes were used and were cut without regard to grain line. The dark contrasting background and border set off the rings. Machine quilting with spider webs and vines covers the surface.

■ Binding the rings along the curves instead of adding a border can emphasize them, but adding a high contrast border can highlight the rings and also give the quilt a "finished" look. Pieced geometric borders complement the curves of the rings.

SOUTHWESTERN, 48" x 48", 1992. A novelty print provided the inspiration for the wild colors in the arcs and corner squares. An inner border and binding of the same ring colors controls the rings while the purple and black borders provide a rest for the eye. The ribboned conchas add some whimsy.

■ The large background areas lend themselves well to appliqué, slashing, weaving, quilting, beading, and other embellishment.

ROSE RINGS, 42" x 53", 1991. A dyed fabric blend from rose to beige makes the rings flow smoothly over the quilt top and into the border making a backdrop for the appliquéd vine and three dimensional roses, buds, and leaves. Heavy stipple quilting was done on the background areas and a vine was quilted into the border. The roses were made with Helma Stewart's methods as shown in the Spring 1991 American Quilter magazine.

IN SEARCH OF A DESIGN
BY KEIKO GOKE

One way of working with a traditional pattern is to draw several blocks of the design, such as the four Double Wedding Ring blocks at left, and then isolate interesting sections. Enlarged, any of these could become an interesting overall design for a quilt, to be developed through Log Cabin piecing or any other technique.

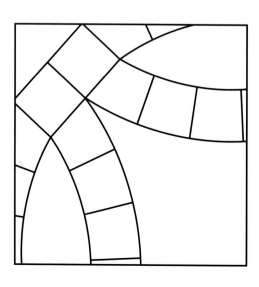

SHIBORI FOR QUILTERS
BY SARA NEWBERG KING

Use shibori to add interesting fabrics to your quilts. This discharge method of shibori involves using a PVC pipe, cotton string, and a bleach bath. Following are brief instructions for the process.

SUPPLIES:
- At least two yards of dark, solid 100% cotton fabric for shibori
- At least one yard each of two other coordinating fabrics
- One foot length of 4" diameter PVC pipe
- 50' of cotton string
- Heavy duty rubber band
- Two plastic bread storage containers or plastic shoe boxes
- Vinyl gloves to protect hands (also wear old clothes)

BASIC INSTRUCTIONS FOR
DISCHARGE SHIBORI

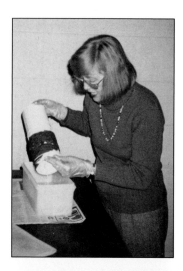

TOP: Submerging wrapped tube in bleach solution.

BOTTOM: Rinsing in clear water.

■ Wearing old clothes, prepare a foot long 4" diameter PVC pipe by cutting a ½" groove into the edge of one end.

■ Prepare 100% dark cotton fabric by cutting it into manageable pieces. I like to work with 12" squares.

■ Fill a plastic shoe box size container with one gallon of cold water and one cup of chlorine bleach.

■ Fill a second container with plain cold water.

■ Tie a knot at the beginning of a 50' cotton string and secure it on the inside of the groove cut into the PVC pipe.

■ Place a corner of the fabric square under the string. Lay the rest of the fabric square around the pipe.

■ Wind the string tightly around the pipe close to the grooved edge on top of the fabric square. Spacing each round of string about one inch apart, tightly wind five more times around the

pipe. Now scrunch those five winds tightly together towards the grooved end of the pipe.

■ Continue winding and scrunching around the pipe as before until you are to the end of your fabric square. You may add other squares in the same manner until the pipe is filled with tightly scrunched fabric.

■ Secure the end of the string with a rubber band so the fabric continues to stay tightly scrunched together.

■ Put on vinyl gloves and gently lower the wrapped pipe into the plastic container containing the bleach bath. Rotate the pipe so that all the fabric is in the solution an equal amount of time (top left).

■ When the fabric has changed color, take the wrapped pipe out of the bleach bath and submerge it in plain water (bottom left).

■ Undo the string and rinse thoroughly. Dry squares and enjoy the designs you have created.

DISCHARGE STENCILING TECHNIQUE
USED FOR RINGS OF THE 90'S

ABOVE: Sara Newberg King uses a bleach solution to stencil rings on her blocks.

LEFT: Stenciled Double Wedding Ring blocks.

PLANNING FABRIC GRAIN FOR MOSAICS
BY NANCY LAMBERT

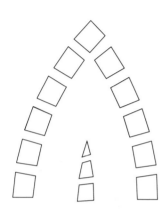

FIG. 1

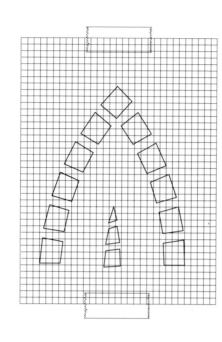

FIG. 2

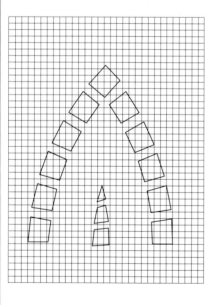

FIG. 3

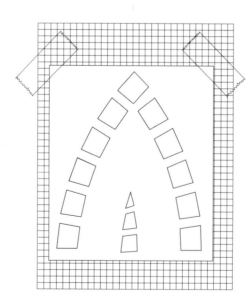

FIG. 4

In order to keep the grain in my mosaic pieces running the same as in the background fabric to which they were being sewn, I developed several handy techniques for transferring graph lines to pattern pieces.

I drew the design on paper and made a photocopy of the design. Fig. 1. Then I taped a piece of Mylar® with graph paper lines over the design. Fig. 2. Next, if I am going to use paper templates, I photocopy the pattern/mylar graph combination on paper. Fig. 3.

If I am going to use a fusible facing like Wonder-Under®, I photo copy the combination onto the Wonder-Under® by taping a piece to plain paper, with the adhesive side towards the paper. Fig. 4. You will need to trace through a few of the graph lines on the interfacing as they will not print well on the fusible web. However these graph lines are transferred, when using the templates, these lines are aligned with the fabric's grain.

The design segment can also be photocopied multiple times on mylar and these segments arranged on graph paper to form the overall pattern. Fig. 5.

Mylar®, graph paper, and a photocopy machine can be used any number of ways to provide guidelines for grain use in mosaics.

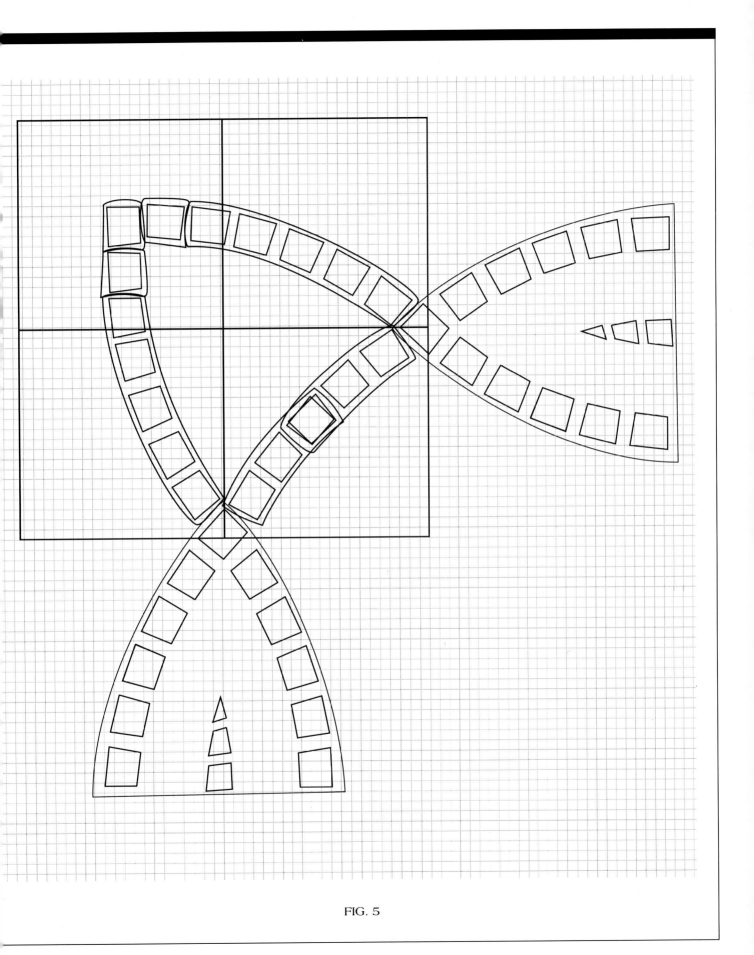

FIG. 5

Patterns from the Quilts

ROYAL WEDDING BLOCK

PIECEFUL SCRAPPERS

Pieces D, Dr, and E are so similar we found it necessary to mark each template with a small circle to indicate the end furthest from the middle of the block.

Within the seam allowance on the fabric pieces, we marked the identifying letter of that piece as well as the small circle. We redrafted G in order to eliminate the seam between blocks. G pieces were stitched in place after all the centers were pieced.

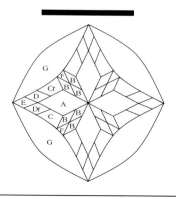

This block is developed from the traditional Chimney Swallows block, as shown in *Scraps Can Be Beautiful* by Jan Halgrimson (Weaver-Finch Publications, PO Box 353, Edmonds, WA 98020)

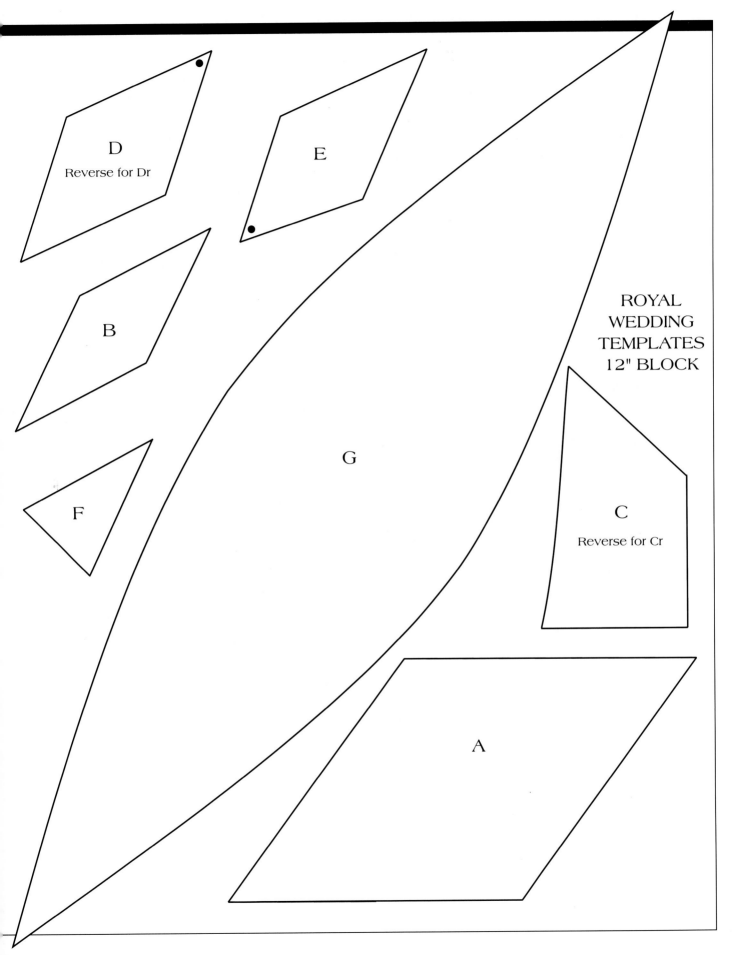

D

Reverse for Dr

E

B

ROYAL
WEDDING
TEMPLATES
12" BLOCK

G

F

C

Reverse for Cr

A

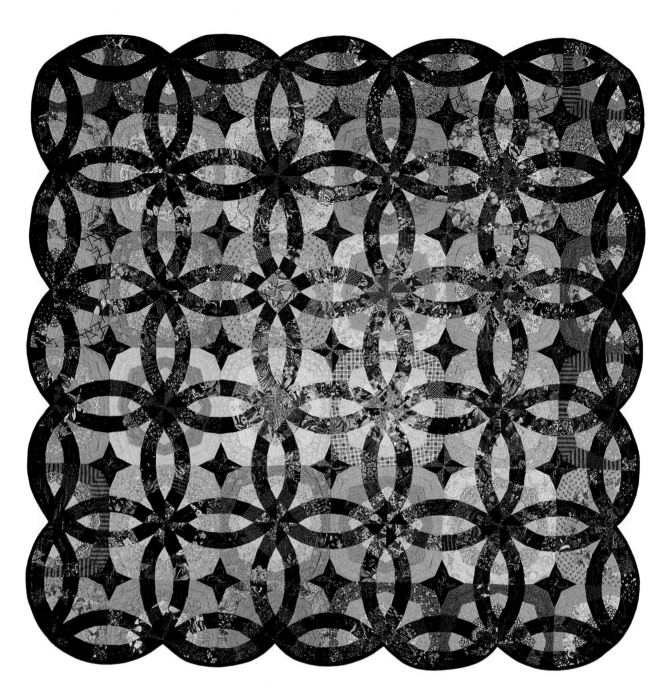

MEDLEY

ELSIE VREDENBURG

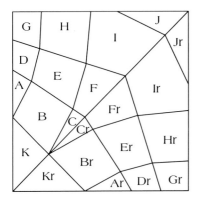

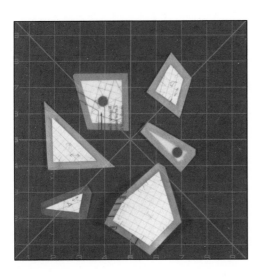

MEDLEY
BY ELSIE VREDENBURG

FABRICS: Assorted scraps. I used pastels in green, blue, pink, and lavender for the background rings (templates A,C,D,F,G,I), and dark jewel tones for the foreground rings (templates B,E,H), teal and purple for the pinwheels (template K), and a lighter teal and fuschia for the stars (template J). All templates need to be reversed for the opposite half of the block.

For each 12" block, cut eight (half in reverse) of each template. See photo of quilt for possible fabric placement. (Exception: the last row of blocks has six of each template, in order to make the scalloped edge).

Stitch together in rows:
    Row 1: A,B,C
    Row 2: D,E,F
    Row 3: G,H, I,J

Stitch rows together, adding K to ABC row. This will give you a right-angle tringle. Using the reverse pieces, stitch the other half of the block. Stitch the two triangles together to form a square. This is one-fourth of the block. Stitch the other three fourths in the same manner. Join the four sections together, with J pieces forming a pinwheel in the center of the block.

Quilting: I quilted (by machine) the background in the ditch with invisible thread, the rings with two colors of metallic thread and a twin needle in a freehand cable design, and the stars in gold metallic thread in a four-petal design.

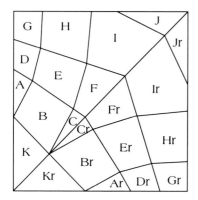

MEDLEY
TEMPLATES
Add seam allowances to all pieces.

Press: left up, right down, center open.
On rings: center row out, end rows in.

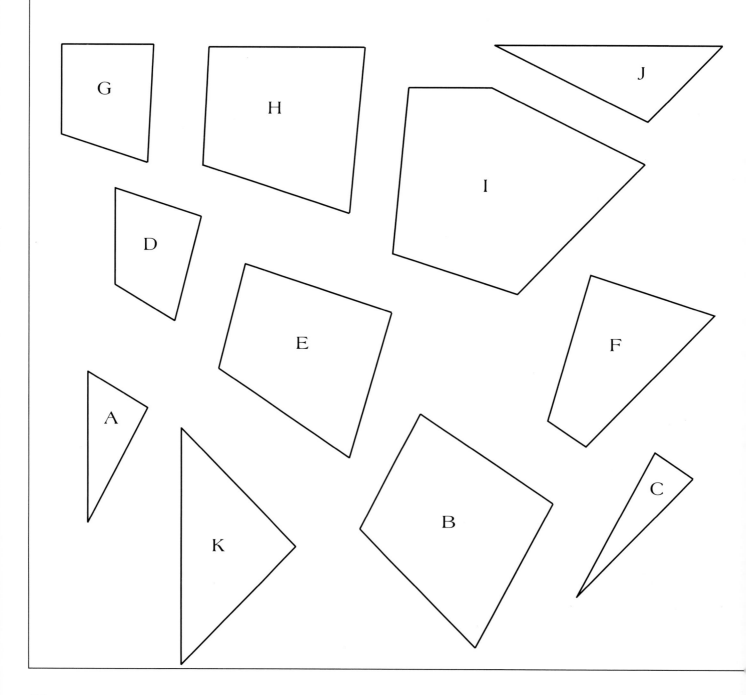

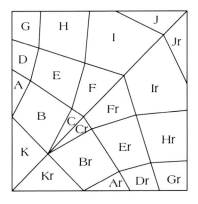

MEDLEY
TEMPLATES
Add seam allowances to all pieces.

Press: left up, right down, center open.
On rings: center row out, end rows in.

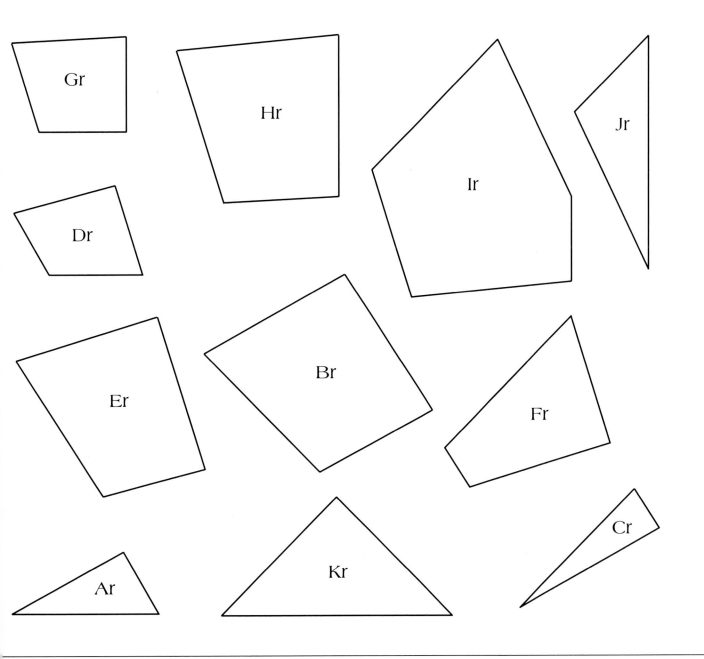

MEDLEY

Plan your own quilt based on this design.

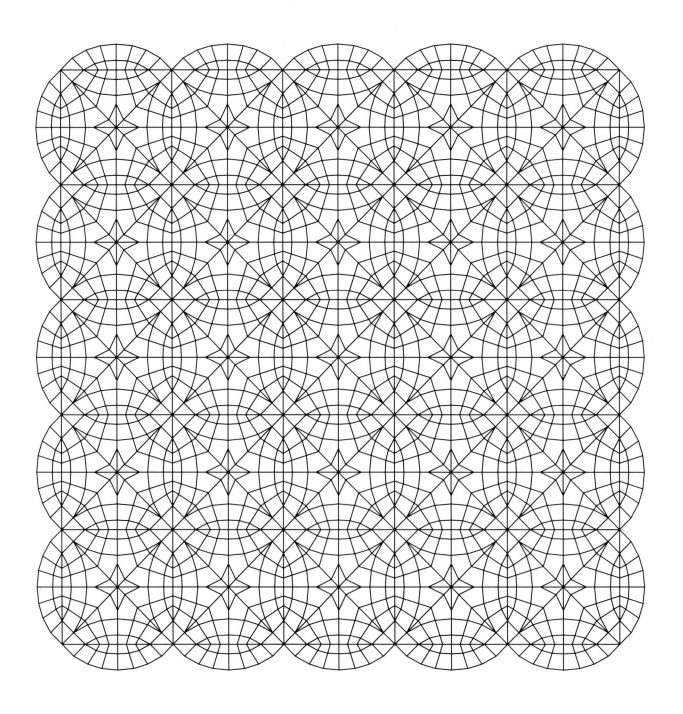

TARANTELLA
BY SYLVIA H. EINSTEIN

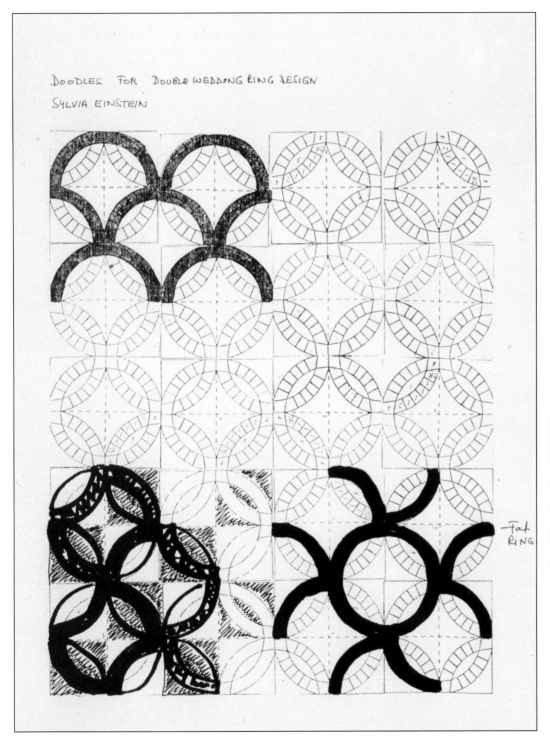

TARANTELLA grew out of many sketches such as these (left). Gradually the block and the overall design developed (below).

©Sylvia Einstein

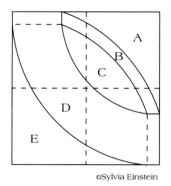

©Sylvia Einstein

TARANTELLA BLOCK
Upper Left Segment

When drawing templates using these segments,
remember to add seam allowances.

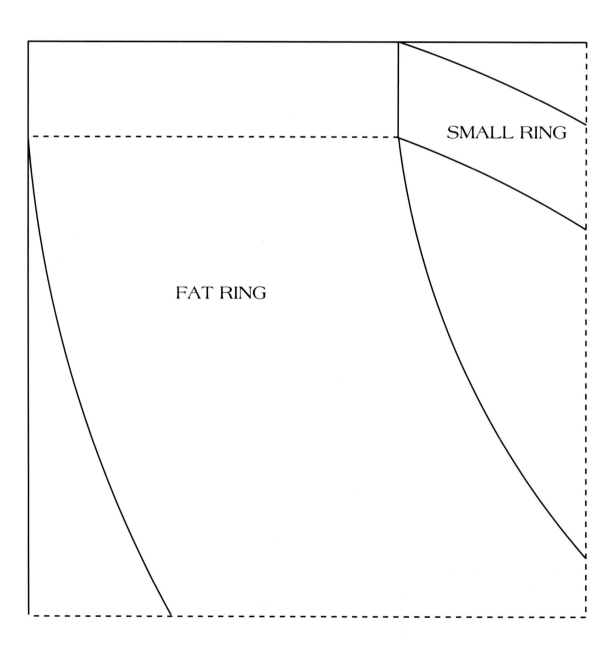

SMALL RING

FAT RING

TARANTELLA BLOCK
Upper Right Segment

When drawing templates using these segments,
remember to add seam allowances.

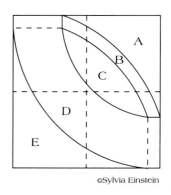

©Sylvia Einstein

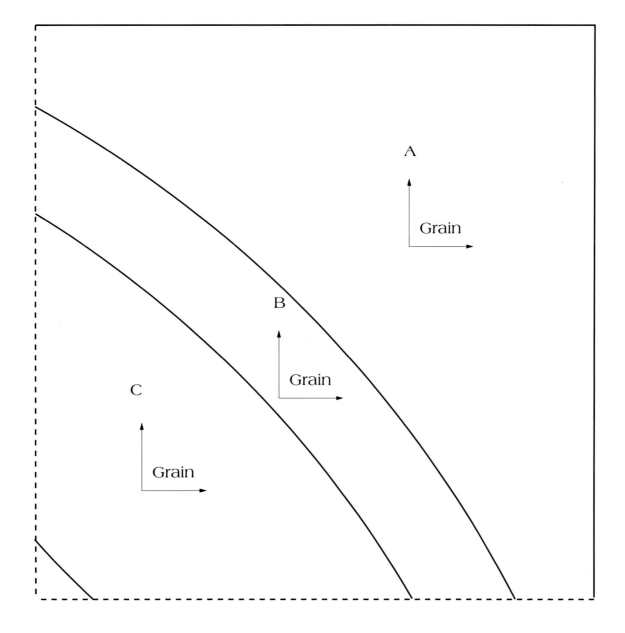

A

Grain

B

Grain

C

Grain

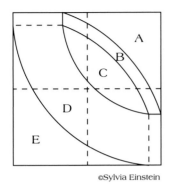

©Sylvia Einstein

TARANTELLA BLOCK
Lower Left Segment

When drawing templates using these segments,
remember to add seam allowances.

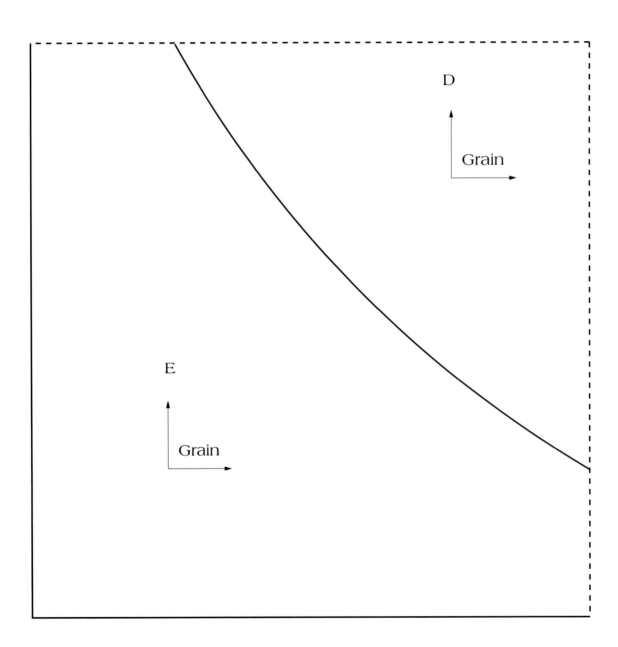

D

↑
Grain
→

E

↑
Grain
→

TARANTELLA BLOCK
Lower Right Segment

When drawing templates using these segments,
remember to add seam allowances.

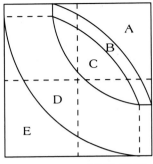

©Sylvia Einstein

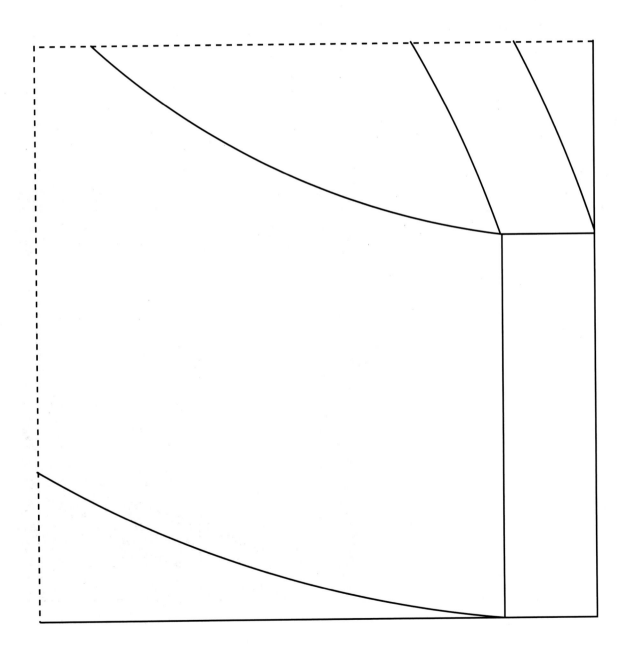

AN EVER-FIXED MARK
BY MARILYN HENRION

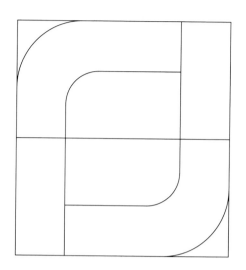

My original design involved a more elongated block like the one shown below right. Ultimately I used the block shown at right. The templates on page 83 can be used to recreate the quilt I made, or you can plan your own using the grid on page 84.

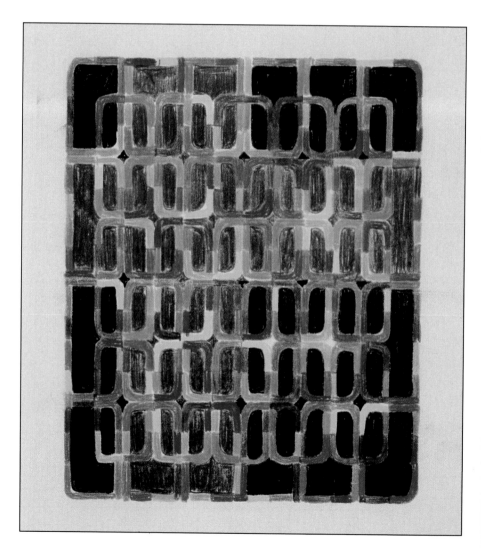

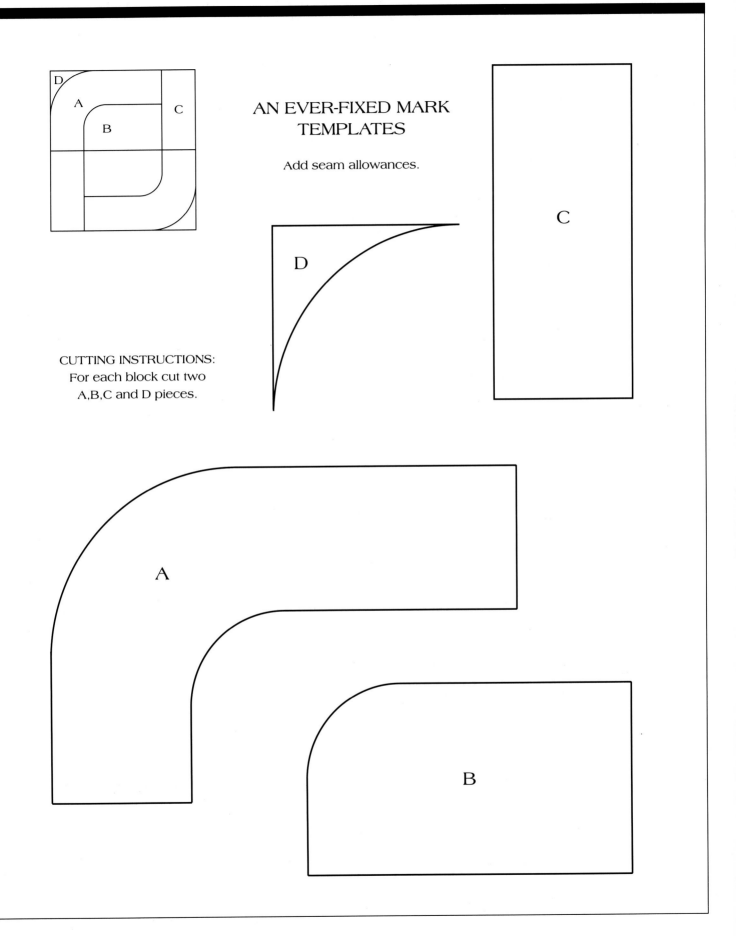

AN EVER-FIXED MARK
TEMPLATES

Add seam allowances.

CUTTING INSTRUCTIONS:
For each block cut two
A,B,C and D pieces.

AN EVER-FIXED MARK

Plan your own quilt based on this design.

LEPRECHAUN WEDDING
DEANNA DEASON DISON

This design was the end result of an extensive series of sketches.

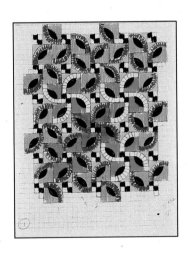

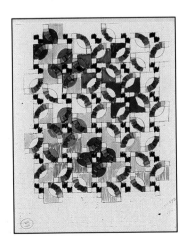

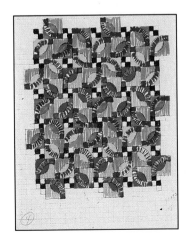

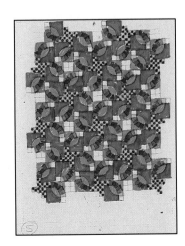

LEPRECHAUN WEDDING

Using the three blocks shown on page 87, this quilt developed.
Use this grid to plan your own quilt based on this design.

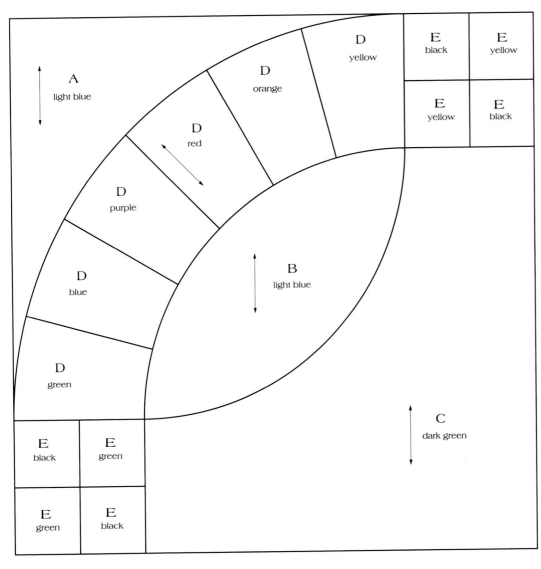

BLOCK DESIGNS

See page 88-89 for full size templates.

E yellow	E black	E yellow	E black
E black	E yellow	E black	E yellow
E yellow	E black	E yellow	E black
E black	E yellow	E black	E yellow

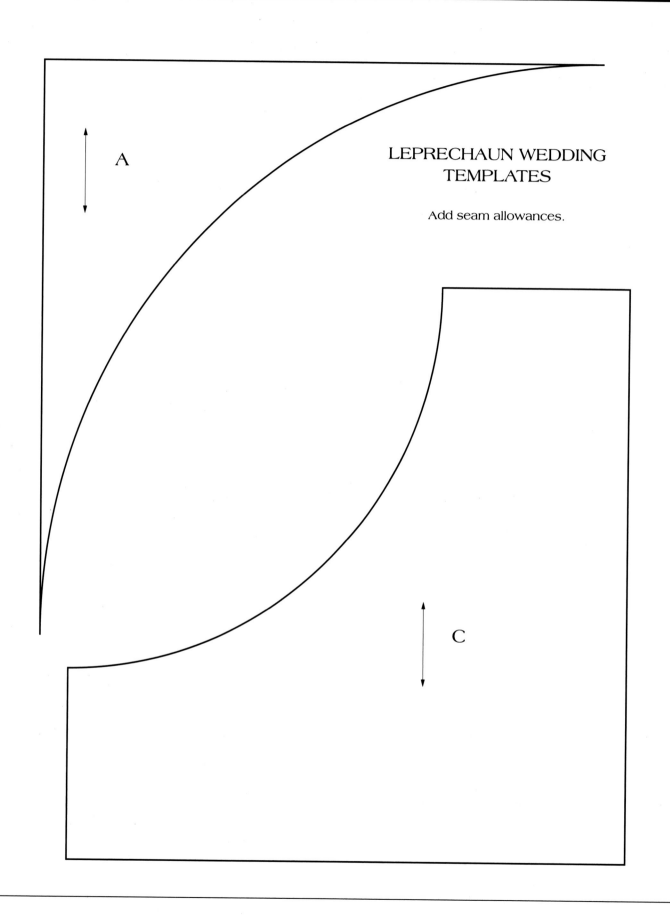

LEPRECHAUN WEDDING
TEMPLATES

Add seam allowances.

A

C

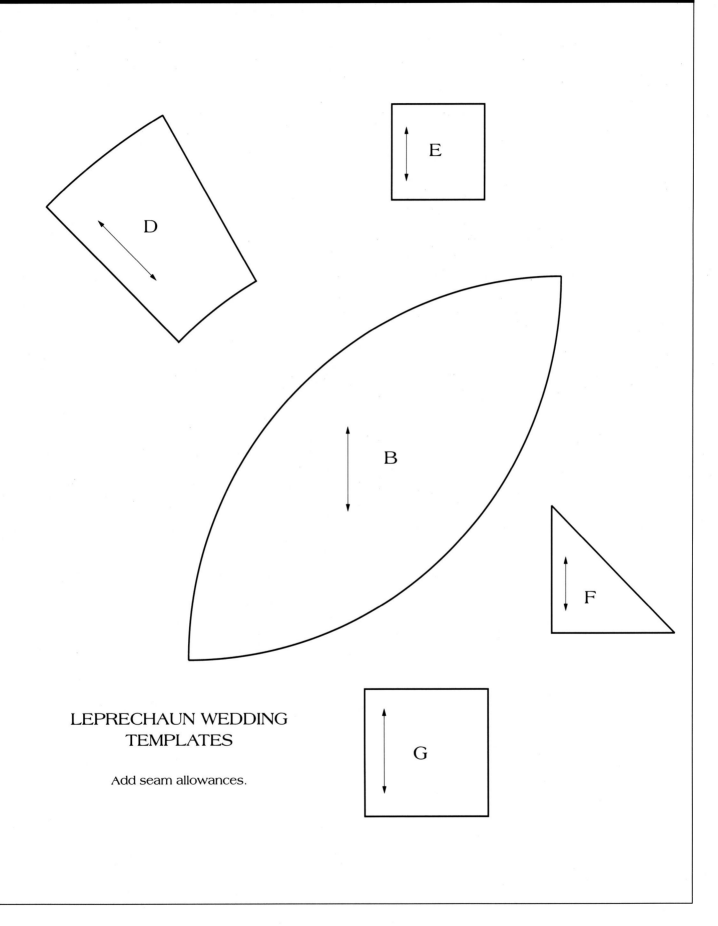

LEPRECHAUN WEDDING
TEMPLATES

Add seam allowances.

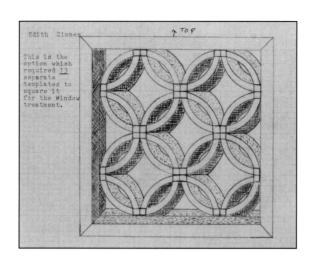

THREE-DIMENSIONAL WEDDING RING WALL QUILT BY EDITH ZIMMER

The sketch at right was the plan I used in developing ATTIC WINDOWS OF MY MIND. I don't usually do this much pre-work, but in this case I wanted to be sure that the design would work before I went to the trouble to cut and piece these blocks.

When other quilters were interested in working with my three-dimensional variation on the Double Wedding Ring pattern, I developed the project sketched above. Unfortunately it took 13 separate templates to square it for the window treatment, and students found it difficult to keep square. I revised the design, creating the four-ring segment shown on page 91. Patterns and instructions for this design follow.

WEDDING RING

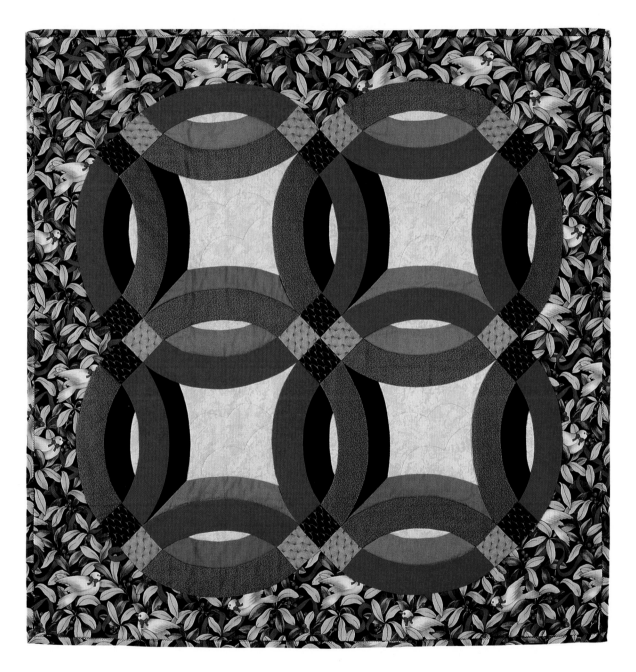

THREE-DIMENSIONAL WEDDING RING WALL QUILT

THREE-DIMENSIONAL WEDDING RING WALL QUILT
EDITH ZIMMER

SUPPLIES:
- Sewing machine and all normal sewing supplies
- Scissors (fabric *and* paper)
- Rotary cutter and pad
- Fine point pen
- Template material (whatever you prefer to use)

FABRICS:
- ½ yard for one set of rings
- ½ yard for second set of rings
- ½ yard for background (light "windows")
- ½ yard *each* of dark and medium solid fabric for shading
- ¼ yard each of two contrasting colors for squares where rings join
- One yard of fabric on which to appliqué completed rings
- ½ yard of the fabric of your choice for the binding

CUT OUT THE FOLLOWING, USING THE TEMPLATES SUPPLIED ON PAGES 98-99:
- A: 12 from background fabric
- B: 6 from dark shading fabric; 6 from medium shading fabric
- C: 12 from ring color number one; 12 from color number two
- D: 12 from square color number one; 12 from color number two
- E: 4 from background fabric
- F: 4 from dark shading fabric
- Fr: 4 from medium shading fabric

Full size templates are on pages 98 and 99.

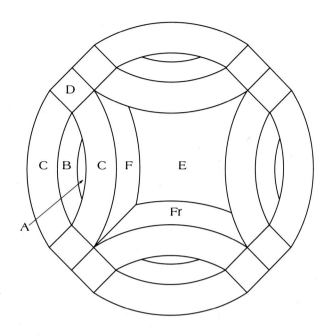

STEP 1

A. Attach six A's to six dark B's

B. Attach six A's to six medium B's

Always be sure to clip all concave curves.

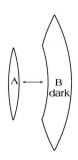

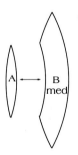

C. Attach 3 of AB units to 3 C's of ring color #1

D. Attach 3 of AB units to 3 C's of ring color #2

E. Attach 3 of AB units to 3 C's of ring color #1

F. Attach 3 of AB units to 3 C's of ring color #2

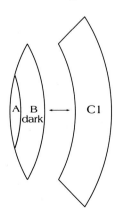

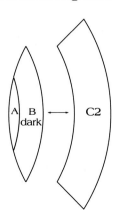

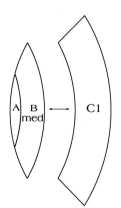

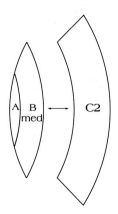

STEP 2

A. Attach 2 D's color #1 to each end of 3 C's ring color #1 and 3 C's ring color #2.

B. Attach 2 D's color #2 to each end of 3 C's ring color #1 and 3 C's ring color #2.

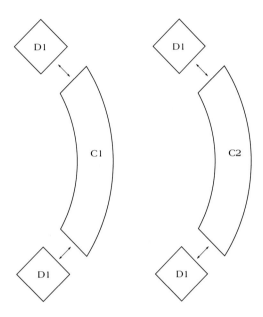

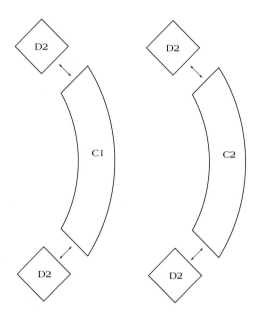

C. Attach these units to the 6 units from STEP 1. These will all have dark B's.

D. Attach these units to the 6 units from STEP 1. These will all have medium B's.

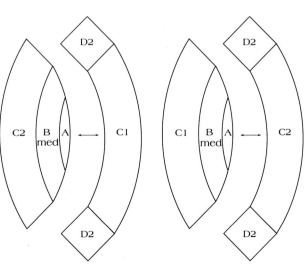

Be sure that the new unit is added to a unit with opposite color C.

STEP 3

Attach F's (dark fabric) to E's. Then attach Fr's (medium fabric) to this unit as below. Make four of these units.

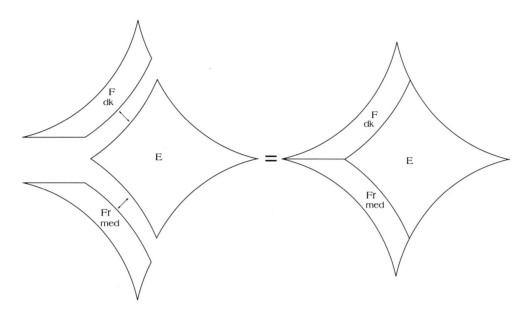

STEP 4

Attach completed units from STEP 2 to units from STEP 3 above. Lay out the units first to be sure you have your arcs placed as shown below. Complete two of each of these units. Note that colors number one and two have been reversed while the dark and medium remain the same. (You will have four arc units left. Do not attach them at this time.)

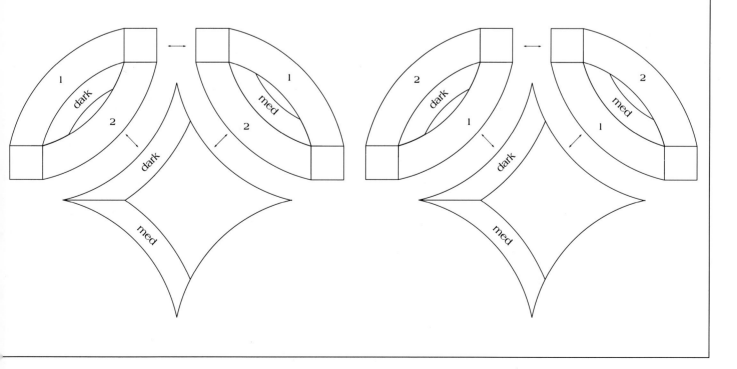

STEP 5

Lay out all units as below. Starting with top unit, attach next two units. Next attach bottom unit, then four remaining arc units.

Your patchwork is now ready to appliqué onto a one yard square of background fabric. If you wish to appliqué the patchwork on point, you will need a square approximately 44" x 44" square.

Use this grid to plan your own quilt using this design.

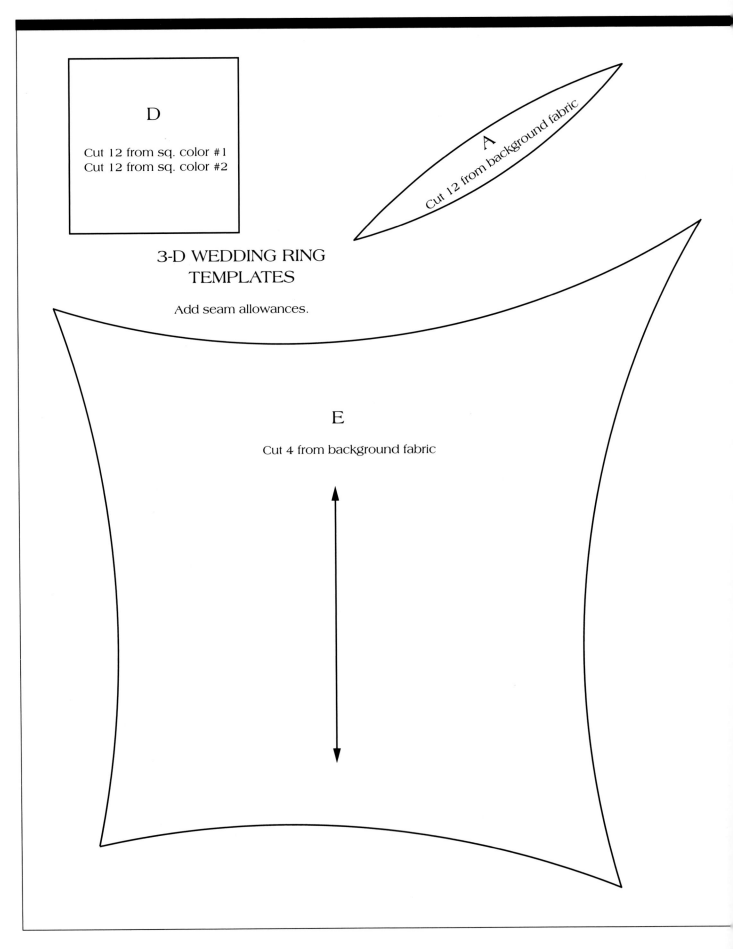

D

Cut 12 from sq. color #1
Cut 12 from sq. color #2

A

Cut 12 from background fabric

3-D WEDDING RING
TEMPLATES

Add seam allowances.

E

Cut 4 from background fabric

3-D WEDDING RING
TEMPLATES

Add seam allowances.

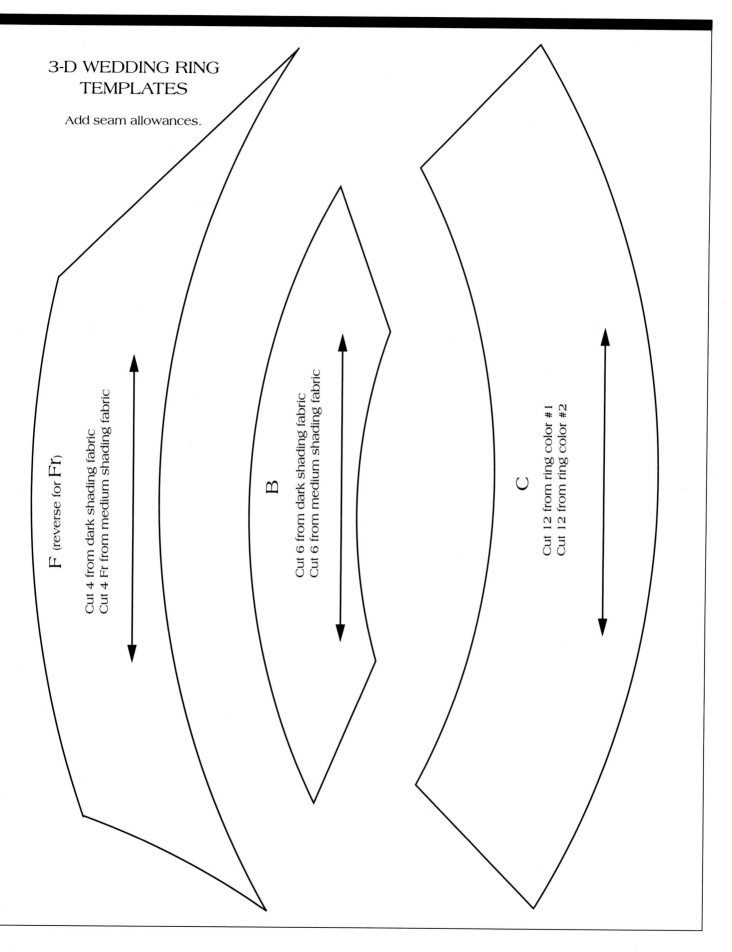

F (reverse for Fr)

Cut 4 from dark shading fabric
Cut 4 Fr from medium shading fabric

B

Cut 6 from dark shading fabric
Cut 6 from medium shading fabric

C

Cut 12 from ring color #1
Cut 12 from ring color #2

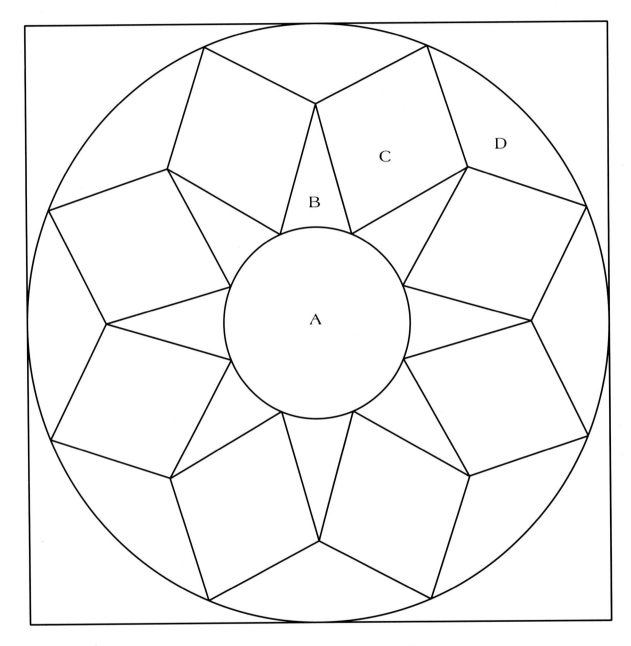

KANSAS SUNFLOWER

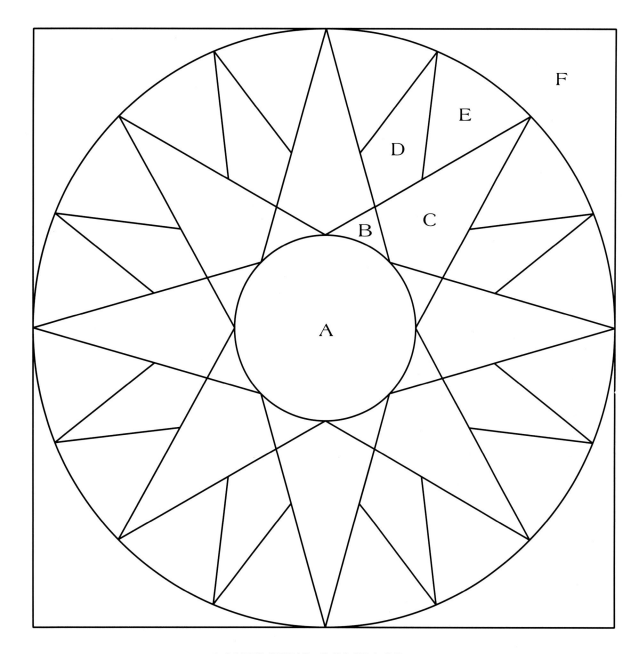

MARINER'S COMPASS

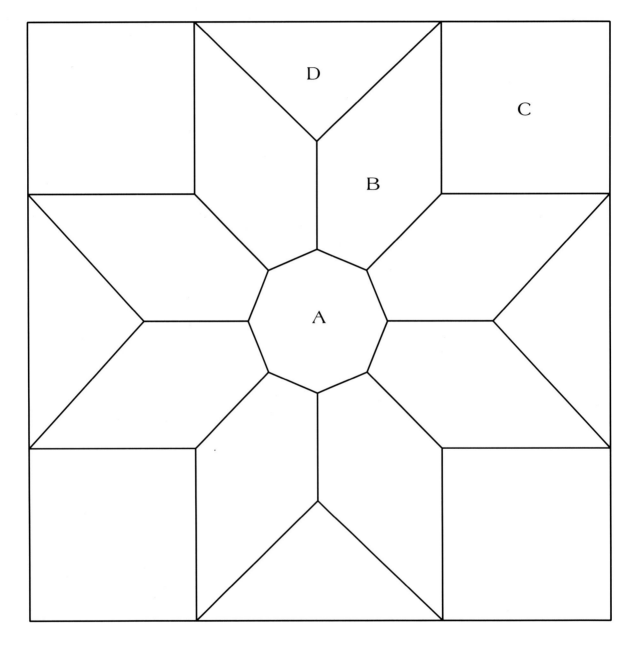

MISSOURI DAISY

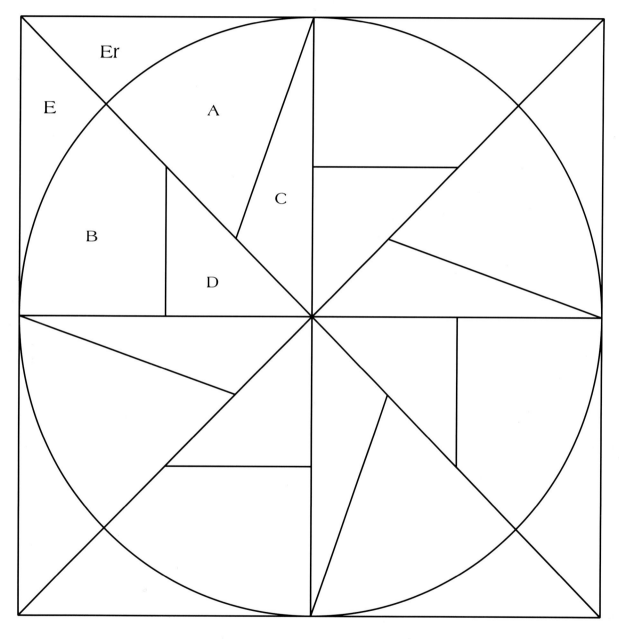

PINWHEEL

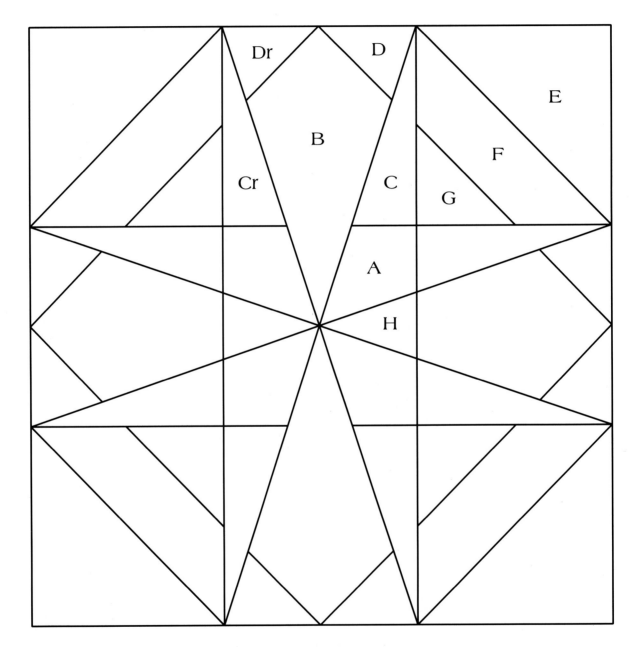

ROLLING ECHOES; CARPENTER'S PUZZLE

JAPAN IN THE ANCIENT MIRROR
QUILTING DESIGNS
BY EMIKO NAGAI

The Quiltmakers

Davis, Shirley Robinson 24-25, 60

Dison, Deanna Deason 22-23, 85-89

Dort, Mildred..26-27, 100-104

Einstein, Sylvia H. 28-29, 77-81

Gilmore-Thompson, Sharon 30-31

Goke, Keiko...14-15, 64

Henrion, Marilyn 20-21, 82-84

Hire, Dianne S. 32-33, 61

King, Sara Newberg..34-35, 65-67

Lambert, Nancy...16-17, 68-69

Lloyd, Jane..36-37

Nagai, Emiko 38-39, 105-107

Ongerth, Marion 40-41

Pieceful Scrappers...42-43, 70-71

Stapleton, Dorothy 44-45

Stein, Susan 18-19, 62-63

Vredenburg, Elsie...46-47, 72-76

Zimmer, Edith...48-49, 90-99

The Quilts

Agony & Ecstasy 24-25

An Ever-Fixed Mark 20-21

Attic Windows of My Mind....................................48-49

Citrus Circuit..36-37

He Was a Kansas Sunflower,
She Was a Missouri Daisy 26-27

Hidden Passion 18-19

Indian Summer...30-31

It's Not All Hearts & Flowers 44-45

Japan in the Ancient Mirror..................................38-39

Medley 46-47

Leprechaun Wedding..22-23

Log Cabin Double Wedding Ring 14-15

Rings of the 90's...34-35

Royal Wedding..42-43

Shotgun Wedding..40-41

Tarantella 28-29

This Is NOT My Grandmother's Wedding Ring,
It Is a NEW Generation of Quilts!...........................32-33

Wedding Ring Mosaics..16-17

The Museum

MUSEUM OF THE AMERICAN QUILTER'S SOCIETY
215 Jefferson Street, Paducah, Kentucky

A dream long held by American Quilter's Society founders Bill and Meredith Schroeder and by quilters worldwide was realized on April 25, 1991, when the Museum of the American Quilter's Society (MAQS, pronounced "Max") opened its doors in Paducah, Kentucky. As is stated in brass lettering over the building's entrance, this non-profit institution is dedicated to "honoring today's quilter," by stimulating and supporting the study, appreciation, and development of quiltmaking throughout the world.

The 30,000 square foot facility includes a central exhibition gallery featuring a selection of the 135 quilts by contemporary quiltmakers comprising the museum's permanent collection, and two additional galleries displaying exhibits of antique and contemporary quilts. Lectures, workshops, and other related activities are also held on site, in spacious modern classrooms. A gift and book shop makes available a wide selection of fine crafts and quilt books. The museum is open year-round and is handicapped accessible.

For more information, write: MAQS, P.O. Box 1540, Paducah, KY 42002-1540 or phone: 502-442-8856.

Other MAQS Publications

Quilts: Old and New, A Similar View

Paul D. Pilgrim and Gerald E. Roy
#3715: AQS, 1993, 40 pages, 8¾" x 8", softbound, $12.95.

New Jersey Quilts – 1777 to 1950:
Contributions to an American Tradition

The Heritage Quilt Project of New Jersey
#3332: AQS, 1992, 256 pages, 8½" x 11", softbound, $29.95.

Quilts: The Permanent Collection – MAQS

#2257: AQS, 1991, 100 pages, 10" x 6½", softbound, $9.95.

The Log Cabin Returns to Kentucky:
Quilts from the Pilgrim/Roy Collection

Gerald E. Roy and Paul D. Pilgrim
#3329: AQS, 1992, 36 pages, 9" x 7", softbound, $12.95.

Nancy Crow: Work in Transition

Nancy Crow
#3331: AQS, 1992, 32 pages, 9" x 10", softbound, $12.95.

These books can be found in the MAQS bookshop and in local bookstores and
quilt shops. If you are unable to locate a title in your area, you can order by mail from:

American Quilter's Society
P.O. Box 3290, Paducah, KY 42002-3290

Please add $1 for the first book and $.40 for each additional one to cover postage and handling.
International orders please add $1.50 for the first book and $1 for each additional one.

To order by VISA or MASTERCARD call toll-free: 1-800-626-5420 or fax: 1-502-898-8890.

~American Quilter's Society~
dedicated to publishing books for today's quilters